LITTLE JADE
MEMOIR OF A YOUNG EURASIAN IMMIGRANT

STIRRED STORIES

LITTLE JADE
MEMOIR OF A YOUNG EURASIAN IMMIGRANT

BY KATHERINE HAAS

To Bob and all whom I've loved, yes, all of you.

"You are forever between that place and this place, dis place and displaced, a site of unease that will always be home. You will never be comfortable anywhere...you always stand inside and outside of any language you encounter..."

Viet Thanh Nguyen
A Man of Two Faces
2023

"Those slender trees held handfuls of soil in their threadlike roots. Cranes bore the wounded giants to deep holes gardeners had prepared in a different spot, and planted them there. The trunks moaned quietly, the leaves drooped in yellow strands, and for a while it seemed that nothing could save them from their agony, but they were tenacious. A slow subterranean rebellion fought to preserve life, vegetal tentacles spread out, blending clumps of dirt from Calle Cueto with new soil. With the inevitable arrival of spring, the palms awoke, swaying from the waist, shaking their hair, rejuvenated despite their trauma. The image of those trees from the home of my ancestors often come to mind when I think of my destiny as an expatriate. It is my fate to wander from place to place, and to adapt to new soils. I believe I will be able to do that because handfuls of Chilean soil are caught in my roots: I carry them with me always."

Isabel Allende
My Invented Country
2003

Contents

The Hsu Family

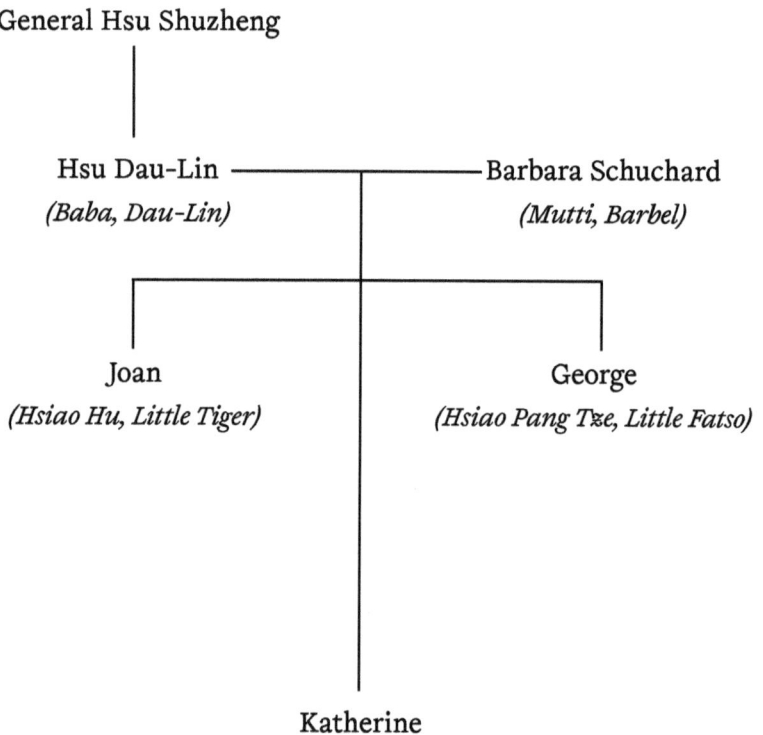

General Hsu Shuzheng

Hsu Dau-Lin ——————————— Barbara Schuchard
(Baba, Dau-Lin) *(Mutti, Barbel)*

Joan George
(Hsiao Hu, Little Tiger) *(Hsiao Pang Tse, Little Fatso)*

Katherine
(Hsiao Yu, Little Jade, Leila Barbara Monika,
Katherine Elizabeth Hsiao Yu Hsu)

Pronunciation Guide

HSIA: she-ah

HSIAO HU: shee-ow hoo

HSIAO PANG TZE: shee-ow pāng dzzuh

HSIAO YU: shee-ow yü

HSU: shü

JIA TONG: geeah tong

Author's Note

All the events I wrote about in this book are true, at least so far as I remember them. What I hope for in the following pages is that the curiosity that has marked my every step comes through. And while my story begins in less culturally aware times, I've tried to convey my lived experiences with respect and empathy.

Some names are invented, like my mother's German friends who hosted us in Hawaii and San Francisco.

CHAPTER ONE

Little Jade

It happened some seventy-plus years ago on a windy May morning, in a country on the other side of the world, but I remember it as if it were yesterday. It was 1949, and I was walking into my fifth-grade classroom in Shanghai, China, with my friend Li Jia Tong when I said, "My father says that Communism would be a horrible outcome for our country." Just as I finished my sentence, Jia Tong noticed Teacher Hsia abruptly putting down her attendance booklet and running over to us. She grabbed me from behind, covered my mouth, and dragged me into the hallway.

I was terrified. A million thoughts went through my head. Were we late for class? Did Teacher Hsia find out about the wrestling match I organized at my home yesterday after school? I knew we weren't allowed to wrestle at school, but I thought it was okay to do it at my house. What had I done wrong? Was I in trouble?

"Hsiao Yu (Little Jade)!" Teacher Hsia almost shouted, although she was trying to whisper. "Don't ever talk about politics. If a classmate overheard you, he might tell his parents. Your father's opinion might get your entire family arrested. Times are dangerous. Civil war is approaching our city. Shanghai could possibly be taken over by Communist forces soon. Do you understand?!"

"Yes, Teacher Hsia," I answered, but I didn't understand, not really. I looked up at my beloved teacher, relieved not to be in trouble and grateful that instead of punishing me, she was trying to keep my family and me safe.

The rest of the school day went fairly well. I shook my head, remembering not to discuss politics with anyone, not even with my best friend Jia Tong. We had become friends earlier in the year during our play rehearsals. We loved to show off in front of others and dramatize everything with our loud voices, so it was no surprise that we were usually given the leading roles.

But my usual propensity to share everything was dampened by Teacher Hsia's warning. I was nervous, and Jia Tong could tell. He handed me my books, smiled and said, "Congratulations on your wrestling championship."

"I didn't win, we tied. He's too big and fat. I couldn't get him down."

"But he couldn't get you down either, and you are a girl and skinny as a rail!"

Just as we approached my house, I saw my five-year-old brother Hsiao Pang Tze peeing into the gutter. At his birth, my mother had asked me to always take care of him. He was my live doll. I rocked him whenever he cried and carried him around. He was so plump at birth that they named him Hsiao

Pang Tze (Little Fatso) to indicate good health. Once he started school, they would give him a more appropriate name. When I admonished him for peeing outside, he insisted that others did it, so why couldn't he. I reminded him that the people who did that were not of our class. They were the "lower class," the uneducated, and the laborers who didn't know any better. Hsiao Pang Tze didn't care.

"I like peeing here, and I get to do whatever I want!" He was right. He was the longed-for beloved son with large eyes, curly hair, and the most adorable smile, which kept him from ever being scolded. Spoiled and pampered by everyone, he acted as if he were a prince. I loved him, but was also jealous. When a friend told me if I kissed my elbow I could change my gender, I spent hours upon hours bending and twisting my elbow, trying to kiss it so I could become a boy and be treated as special too.

Leaving Hsiao Pang Tze playing with his friends in our backyard, I heard my fifteen-year-old sister Hsiao Hu practicing the piano. Her nimble fingers flew over the keyboard as she produced heavenly sounds that the cooks and housekeepers enjoyed as well as the rest of us. She excelled in everything.

She was popular at school, brilliant academically, and looked like a tiny porcelain doll possessing exquisite delicate features with lustrous wavy hair. Everyone admired her, and I was filled with envy. My features were plain, I had straight hair, and I did not learn quickly in school.

Once home, I puzzled over Teacher Hsia's comment all afternoon. I was eager for dinner when the family gathered and there would be a chance for me to ask questions.

My father (Baba) Hsu Dau-Lin was the second son of high-ranking General Hsu Shuzheng, who was a major figure at the time when China changed from the dynastic rule of emperors to become a republic. Baba was bright, so he was chosen to be educated at home with elderly tutors from the tender age of three. My grandfather Hsu Shuzheng conquered Mongolia in 1919, and wanted this son, Dau-Lin, to carry on the tradition of devoting his life to China.[1] So in 1925 at the age of eighteen, Baba was sent from China to France and then Germany, to study for his PhD in international law.

In Germany, Baba discovered the joy of studying with young scholars instead of serious old men. He was overjoyed to be able to spend time with intellectual equals, most of whom were Jewish. Among these friends, his best friend, Stephan Kuttner, introduced Baba to my beautiful mother, Barbara Schuchard. They dated for close to a year before marrying.

My mother (Mutti), Barbara Schuchard, had been a strong student in high school. She had once acted the lead in a well reviewed production of Shaw's Saint Joan. Then one day her teacher asked her to correct some test papers, handing Mutti a stack and saying to her, "Mark many errors on these papers, regardless of whether the answers are correct or not. They are papers of your Jewish classmates." Mutti was furious. She saw herself as a champion of those in need, and would always strive for justice. So, she went home and quit school altogether. But then another teacher came to her home and told her about a better school to which Mutti would have to take a train across town. This would be an improved environment for my mother,

---

[1]Hsu Shuzheng was a Chinese warlord. In 1919, Hsu Shuzheng took command of the Chinese Northwest Frontier Defense Army and invaded what is now the modern day country of Mongolia. He briefly brought the region back under control of the Chinese, until 1921, when the region regained its independence from China.

and among the primarily Jewish kids there Mutti became best friends with her classmate Eva Illch.

By 1933, Eva married Stephan Kuttner and moved to Rome. When Baba completed his PhD in law, he returned to China to work as a high-level appointee to General Chiang Kai-shek. He wrote to Mutti proposing marriage, who was just then seething at recent Nazi actions that would enable them to take over the government of Germany. Barely a month earlier she passed a store where an elderly Jewish woman was trying to buy something, and two Nazis prevented her from entering. Mutti shoved the Nazi soldiers aside and helped the woman enter. These Nazis then grabbed Mutti and forced her into a car. They took her to a basement somewhere to be interrogated.

"What is your name? Where do you live? What do your parents do? Why were you helping the Jewish lady?"

This frightened my nineteen-year-old mother. When they were discussing her fate, a young Nazi came over to her sitting there and whispered, "If you want to live, young lady, *keep your mouth shut.*"

As a result of what she endured, my mother decided to make the trip to China just to see if she really wanted to marry Baba–although her father Theodore cautioned her, "You see one Chinese and think he is cute, but when you see a billion, you'll learn that he is no longer that cute."

On the ship to China, many passengers found out my mother was going to marry a Chinese man and urged her not to marry him. They collected enough money for her to buy a passage back to Germany, but she declined to go. When Mutti arrived in China, she discovered that marriage plans were already underway and she was too embarrassed to say, "Wait, I need time to think about this." So, my parents were married in 1933, about the same time as their best friends Stephan Kuttner and Eva. A year later, my sister arrived.

Born on the evening of a powerful storm, they named her Hsiao Hu (Little Tiger). As she grew, she showed not only physical strength, but also a strong will, and she spoke loudly and confidently. Baba thought perhaps if they changed the word "Hu" slightly by adding a radical to the written character, it would still sound the same but it would mean, "amber," a beautiful jewel, and she might grow up to be more ladylike, demure, and quiet. It didn't work.

When Hsiao Hu was three, Mutti became pregnant with me. Our family was in Nanking, the capital of China at the time, in 1937 when the Japanese were about to invade. My father sent my sister and Mutti back to Mutti's home in Germany where they'd be safe during the invasion that ultimately became the Nanking Massacre.[2] That December, while Nanking and its people were suffering incredible destruction and brutality, I was born in a hospital in Berlin.

When I was born, the doctor told Mutti that I had jaundice. My mother laughed, "Doctor, she is Chinese, that is why she is yellow. You just have never seen a Chinese baby before." In spite of this the doctor assured her that I had jaundice, and that my yellow skin color was not because I was Chinese.

And as for my name? When the nurse asked my mother what name she should put on my birth certificate, my mother said,

---

[2] The Nanjing Massacre, also called the rape of Nanjing, was the murder of many Chinese civilians in Nanjing by the Imperial Japanese Army, in the Second Sino-Japanese War. The mass killings started in December 1937, and carried on for six weeks. It's estimated that anywhere from 100,000 to more than 300,000 people died.

"This child doesn't need a German birth certificate, because we are going back to China soon." But the German hospital insisted on Mutti filling out the form, including my name, before she was allowed to leave with me. Mutti gave the form to my grandmother Leah to fill in any name she wanted. Mutti never even asked what my grandmother named me.

In July 1938, Baba was appointed by Chiang Kai-shek to be Acting Ambassador to Rome. His job was to represent China in discussions with the Italian government. So, Mutti took Hsiao Hu and me to Italy to join my father. We lived there in a palace, which, rumor has it, someone had given to Mussolini as a bribe. Mussolini sold that palace to the Chinese government because he didn't find the bribe enticing. During those four turbulent years in Rome, I was known as "Baby" because they thought we'd be going back to China any day and figured there would be time enough when we returned to give me a Chinese name.

The palace in which Katherine's family lived while in Italy

The Hsu family posing for an immigration photo

In 1942, our family did move back to China. We were in Chongqing, the war capital. There I received my Chinese name,

Hsiao Yu (Little Jade). My parents thought perhaps with a jewel name from the beginning of life, I might grow up to be calm, quiet, and poised. As with Joan, it didn't work for me either.

In Chongqing, Baba was in Chiang Kai-shek's cabinet until the end of World War II, when we moved to Shanghai. So the first few years of my life, I shuttled from Berlin, to Rome, and to Chongqing, ultimately landing in Shanghai.

Although my father worked as a highly regarded dean of a law school in Shanghai, he was a gentle, easy-going, kind father at home. He teased us often and praised us occasionally even though that was not how the Chinese typically treated their children back then. For example, I taught myself to stand on a large barrel lying sideways in our backyard and to roll it with my feet without losing my balance. He loved that, and commended me for it. What was ironic was that my German mother acted more like a Chinese parent, comparing us to one another, criticizing us frequently in order to encourage us.

That evening I was anxious for my parents to ease my mind. As soon as our family sat down at the dining room table, before all the dishes had been brought in, I said, "Teacher Hsia told me today that it is dangerous to talk about politics at school because there is a civil war. I don't understand..."

When the servants finished bringing in the steaming supper dishes redolent of fish and meats, my Baba spoke softly, "Your teacher is right. Many people believe that Communism would be wonderful for our country because everything would be fair. The government would make sure that there would be no rich people and no poor ones either. They plan to take away much of the extra things the rich have and give them to the poor, so all people would be equal."

Well, that sounded like a great idea. How could Baba be against that? Almost every day I would see beggars going through our garbage cans outside, looking for any scrap of food that might cling to an apple core or a bone. Often, on my way to school, I'd walk past someone on the sidewalk who had died of cold or hunger during the night. Some beggars even blinded their children because more people would give money to a blind child than a sighted one.

Hsiao Hu joined in, "It seems unfair, Baba, that we own three houses, but outside we see homeless people. You are sending me to a fancy boarding school where I am learning incredibly interesting subjects. Yet right outside one can see children wandering around not having the resources to attend school or even enough money for warm clothing or shoes."

"We buy tanks of warm water delivered to our home to fill our bathtub each week!" Hsiao Pang Tze joined in. "And I get to wash right after Baba and Mutti! The kids outside probably don't wash once a week in any water."

I thought about that comment. Yes, my little brother gets to wash in that water right after my parents, then my sister and by the time it is my turn, the water is no longer hot, nor clean. If only I could kiss my elbow, then I could bathe in clean and warm water without soap scums floating around! "Oh, well," I thought, at least I am able to have a bath, whereas many others don't have the privilege.

My parents felt differently about the issue. Mutti turned to us, "Do you think it would be fair to take away the houses Baba worked hard for just to give it away to others who didn't do anything to deserve it?"

I sat quietly to think that over. But Hsiao Hu asked, "How did this difference of opinion escalate into a civil war?"

Baba explained Communism's origins as we pondered.

"Yes, the two factions fought the Japanese together, but split apart afterwards. My boss, General Chiang, was not a great leader, and many were disappointed in him. Mao Zedong began to gather many followers shortly after the war. Now they have been successful in starting a civil war, and seem to be winning."

"Communism seems like a good idea," Baba continued, "but it doesn't work. The government of the Soviet Union tried it and it just doesn't work. When every worker is paid the same amount whether they work very hard or very little, soon almost everyone decides there is no point in working hard, and production rates drop. When the pay is equal, no one wants to do the hard jobs; everyone wants the easy ones. Communism seems like a perfect system, but it isn't. Half of the country is fighting the other half. The people on our side, the Republic, believe that people should be paid according to how well they do their job. They believe that those who don't work hard should be fired. But the Republic side is losing. You children and your mother may have to leave the country."

Hsiao Hu sat up and shouted, "What? Why?" All three of us kids stopped eating, dropped our chopsticks and our rice bowls, and stared at Baba and Mutti. Panic covered our faces and hearts.

"If the Communists take over, your mom and you three will be in danger. They are blaming many of China's ills on the foreigners. It was foreign countries that brought opium to China and drugged our people. When we tried to stop them, they brought their warships to fight against us and won. The

Communists want revenge against the foreigners. Your lives would be in danger if they won."

"But we are Chinese!" Hsiao Hu, Hsiao Pang Tze, and I shouted in protest.

"In their eyes, you three are half-German, which means you are foreigners."

"But where would we go?" Little Hsiao Pang Tze asked. His face, usually so cheerful, looked distressed.

Baba sighed, "Maybe the United States of America. Our good friends, the Kuttners, live in Washington, D.C. and they have offered to host our family for as long as it is needed. However, Americans don't want more Chinese people in their country. We might try to get you three passports under Mutti's German citizenship."

That year, a while before America adopted a more liberal immigration system, only 105 Chinese were allowed to enter as permanent residents.

"Wouldn't you come with us?" I asked.

"No," Baba said, lowering his shoulders and sighing, "I can't abandon my country. I was raised to lead it." The idea of leaving Baba behind frightened me. He was the one who held me in his lap when company came, telling them that I was his favorite child. It was marvelous. Baba's affection made me feel as charming or intelligent as my siblings.

"If we left, how long would we be away?" Hsiao Hu demanded. She was the brave one.

"You would stay only a short while," Baba assured us, "the Communists can't control China for long."

As dinner went on, every time a servant came in to bring a dish or pour tea, or take bowls and plates, all conversation ceased. The servants did not earn much money, but they had a place to stay and food to eat. "They would probably think that a Communist government would make their lives better," I thought. "Teacher Hsia was right. Baba seems not to trust even our dear servants who have been living with us for years."

That night in bed, I thought about the dinner conversation, and that led me to a lot of questions and worries. America? I thought about what it would mean to go to a country that spoke such a weird and different language. In school I had some English classes and learned to say a few words and phrases, like "Hello, how are you? I am well, thank you." We also learned to sing a song or two in English, but that was all. The one American teacher we had had left several months ago. We presented a play to honor her and I was chosen to play her. Probably because I looked Western. Even though I loved performing this part, it felt weird to be dressed up as an American. If we went to America, would I have to wear funny clothes like that all the time?

Lying in bed, I was sure that going to America would be horrible. I thought back to seven years prior when we had to leave Italy and move to China. The palace in Rome where our family had lived for almost four years was magnificent. I spoke French to my French-Swiss governess and Italian to everyone else, including the guard, the maids, the cooks, the butler, the gardener, and the chauffeur. Leaving that home, that country, was upsetting for all of us.

When we first moved to China, our house in Chongqing could not be more different than the palace in Rome. We left behind life-sized dolls, not to mention two huge pet tortoises in the garden there, which included twenty-seven fountains. There was a marble staircase that Hsiao Hu slid down when no one was looking. But in Chongqing our house was small, without any electricity or running water. The toilet we had was a bucket we squatted in.

There were no toys, and I had two new languages to master: Mandarin, which my parents and Hsiao Hu spoke fluently, and the Chongqing dialect, which had no sounds in common with Mandarin. The only soothing part of Chongqing was finally meeting my Chinese grandmother, whom I loved and who adored me. Beyond that, the adjustment was very difficult for me; I longed for the comforts of our palace where I'd felt warm and cozy.

When Baba and Mutti tried to enroll me in kindergarten in Chongqing, I failed the entrance test and had to wait a year to be accepted. The entrance test consisted of three questions:

1. What comes at night and steals things?

I answered a mouse, which was wrong because they wanted me to say a thief.

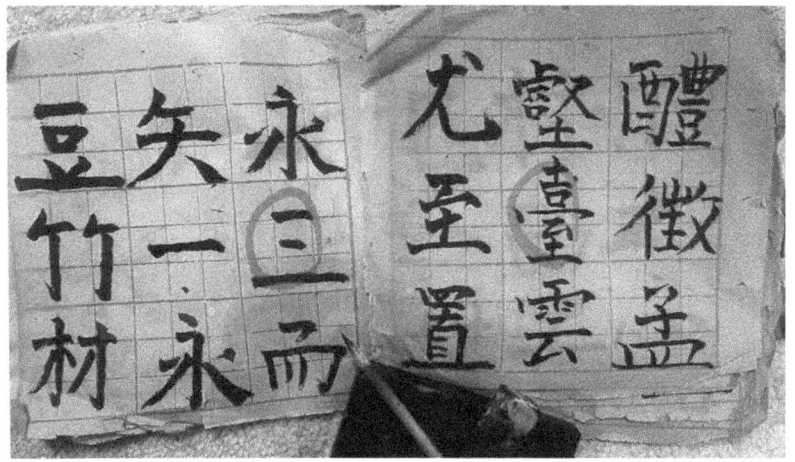

Katherine's childhood writing book

2. What is a Chinese writing brush made of?
I said bamboo, but that was just its handle. They wanted me to say goat, weasel, or rabbit fur, which were used for writing.
3. Who is Confucius?
I knew nothing about Confucius, the great Chinese philosopher who guided the Chinese. I was just learning to speak Mandarin and the Chongqing dialect, while trying to forget Italian and French, which muddled my brain.

That year was my worst year yet. Four years later, after moving to Shanghai from Chongqing, I had finally mastered Mandarin and the dialect from the Shanghai region. Now, moving to America would mean another language–English. It would mean leaving behind my beloved Baba, which was an unbearable thought. It would mean leaving my grandmother and friends. Would I have to go through another experience like the one before? From my bed, I looked at the evening star, the first star seen in the sky, and wished fervently that the civil war would end quickly and that we would not have to leave. Ever. This is my country, my people, my language. I needed a plan.

Maybe just wishing really hard would work. In the Chinese translation of *Pinocchio*, I read that Geppetto wished upon a star and his puppet Pinocchio came to life. But there was no blue fairy to help me here. Wishing had sort-of worked, however, when I wished on the first star I saw to win the wrestling championship I'd organized. Wishing had also worked four months earlier when I wished for Jia Tong to walk me to and from school, and he did. Wishing for the civil war to end quickly became my plan. I fell asleep happy and hopeful.

One afternoon a week later, when I came home from school, Mutti seemed to be in a tizzy. My sister Hsiao Hu was packing a small suitcase. Mutti was packing my little brother's suitcase. On my bed was another suitcase, opened and empty.

"We are going on a trip," Mutti said, "Pack your important things."

"Where are we going? School isn't over until the middle of June," I asked, hoping we were NOT headed to the United States of America.

"Just a little trip, hurry up and pack, we leave in a half hour."

I thought about what was important. I didn't want to get behind in school. Catching up with my classmates in Shanghai after two school years in Chongqing had been awful. So, I packed all my school books, writing notebook, brushes and ink stick, and my ink slate, so that I could practice calligraphy. That way I could work on my own and when we returned from our trip, I wouldn't be behind. Teacher Hsia would be pleased to see that I kept up with the homework even when away on vacation.

Mutti put on her winter coat to leave. I wondered why she chose that coat, since it was too warm outside for it. What we didn't know was that Mutti had sewn her jewels inside the lining of her coat. Immigrants were not allowed to bring large sums of money or jewels on a visiting visa to the U.S. But Mutti could sell the precious diamonds, pearls, and emeralds to generate emergency funds in case we needed them.

Our driver took us to the dock, with Baba sitting in the front seat with him. Mutti, my sister, my brother, and I sat in the back. The evening sun was about to set and hundreds of people were milling around. We got out of the car and pushed through the crowd with our suitcases to get to our ship. Chinese do not hug or kiss in public, but Mutti hugged Baba. I had never seen them hug or kiss before. Ever. In fact, about three months earlier, Mutti had taken Hsiao Hu and me to see a foreign film. In the middle of the movie, the male star kissed his girlfriend. When I saw that, I shouted, "Why is he biting her?" causing the audience to roar with laughter. My sister had to explain to me that the actors were kissing.

With heaviness in everyone's demeanor, we said goodbye. I held on to Baba's hand as hard as I could. I didn't want to go, and I didn't want him to stay behind. He smiled with tears welling, rubbed my head and pushed me towards Mutti and my siblings, who seemed excited about a trip on such a huge ship. Boarding the USS General Gordon, a troop carrier America had sold to the Chinese after World War II, we took our suitcases and found our cabin. It was filled with bunk beds for the many other passengers with whom we'd have to share the space. Crammed in the ship were over a thousand people. I told myself the trip was temporary—we'd be back soon, very soon.

Our family went out on the deck with all the other passengers. As the ship pulled away from the dock, many people tossed long colorful streamers of paper, which flew off the side of the ship towards families and friends waving goodbye. The ship blew its horns to announce our departure. Baba watched as his family waved and waved—eyebrows furrowed, tears welling, the distance between us and him ever increasing. We would not see him again until we were all grown.

CHAPTER TWO

I Get a New Name

The next morning, I felt seasick and I could barely get up. The rocking ship made me feel as if everything in my stomach was about to rise up and land on the floor of our cabin. Hsiao Hu and Hsiao Pang Tze were already up, ready to eat and explore the ship. I forced myself to get up, and the three of us headed for the dining room for breakfast where Mutti was waiting.

As we were eating our scrambled eggs and toast, I noticed a Chinese man across from us. He sat there looking and looking at the fried egg and toast on his plate. The poor man had obviously never eaten Western food and had no idea what to do. He was used to using chopsticks to pick up the vegetables and meat, placing them in his rice bowl, lifting the bowl to his lips and shoveling the contents into his mouth. But now the food was already on his plate, and how was he going to get it from the plate into his mouth? Finally, he bent his face down to the table and began to shovel the contents toward his mouth with the fork that he held awkwardly with his fist. But before he took a bite, he sat up quickly. He then lifted the entire plate up to his mouth with one hand and tried to shovel the egg with the fork into his mouth. He quickly set the plate down once again, probably thinking that this couldn't be right, either. So once more, he bent down then sat up quickly, bringing the plate to his mouth to try and shovel the egg into his mouth, but again, he set the plate down without eating the egg. He went through this routine three or four times. With a loud sigh, he finally bent over and shoveled the egg into his mouth in one big gulp. His face was red with shame. "Why didn't he look around to see how others were eating breakfast?" I wondered.

I managed to eat my breakfast without any issues, but it did not sit well. The ship's constant rocking made me lose it within a half hour. I spent the next two days in bed, eating next to nothing and wishing we were home.

I had so many worries about what was happening at home without us. I wondered if Baba was feeding the white cat with four kittens under our porch. I wondered what Jia Tong thought when he rang my doorbell to walk me to school and heard from our servants that we had left. I wondered who would get the main part in the play that Teacher Hsia assigned to me last Thursday. I wished that this was all a nightmare and I'd soon wake up.

I worried a lot about the four young neighborhood boys who came to our house for reading and writing lessons every afternoon. Before I started lessons with them, these children had been playing in the streets all day, because education was available only for those who paid for it. I wanted to give back to those around me who didn't have the same access as I had. And so I decided to spend my afternoons teaching them. About a year ago, Teacher Hsia had given me a small black board and chalk as well as some spare schoolbooks to use during my lessons. When I first started teaching the neighborhood boys, Hsiao Hu got upset and asked, "Why are you letting these ragamuffins into our bedroom?!" She saw them as bringing dirt into our home. I convinced my sister by telling her that I'd clean up after they left.

I loved the little classes that I taught daily to these children. After a few months of classes, the father of one young boy was so impressed with his son's reading skills, he promised to save enough to send him to school the next year. That made me happy, though I remembered another boy in my class who was beaten for coming and learning words. He was forbidden to join us again. I suspected his father worried that this boy might ask to attend school and the cost was beyond the ability of his father, who earned just enough to support his family.

On May 7, 1949, after three days in bed, I finally got over my seasickness. I woke up hungry and eager to explore the ship with my siblings. The three of us went up to the top and looked out at the ocean. There were ropes everywhere. Little Pang Tze wondered what the ropes might be for as he climbed up on them. Out on the ocean, we marveled at all kinds of interesting sea creatures. I wanted to scoop them up and keep them in a bowl as pets. We watched as a giant sea turtle flipped over, with water splashing way up. That was a sight to remember. To pass the time, sometimes we would look at the passengers and make jokes about them. We all knew it was not polite, but maybe no one noticed.

A few days later, the ship stopped at the port of Manila. We had never been to the Philippines and it was so much fun watching the crew unload cargo and reload other goods bound for America. I wished we were allowed to get off and explore the city while the sailors were working. The captain was gathering all the food that would be needed for the twenty-four-day trip to the United States. Suddenly, my sister Hsiao Hu noticed a nearby ship and a handsome merchant marine sailor on it who was smiling at her. She smiled back. They waved at one another.

"Elder sister," I cautioned, "Don't encourage him. I saw Mutti slapping you for flirting. I think she worries about you."

The General W.H. Gordon, pictured during the Hsu family voyage, was the last ship to leave Shanghai before its fall to the Communist regime.

Hsiao Hu ignored me and told me to take Hsiao Pang Tze down to the lower deck to play shuffleboard. She stayed there, trying to communicate with the sailor using hand signals. As evening approached, the young sailor sent a message in Morse code asking for her name. My sister didn't understand Morse code, so she approached the sailor who was operating the lights on our ship and coyly asked him to blink a message back to the sailor on the adjacent ship. The signalman on our ship was delighted to help these youngsters flirt, and relayed her messages. Hsiao Hu told me all this that evening when Mutti was busy chatting with her new friends.

That evening at supper Mutti announced, "Since we are going to be living in America, you will all need new names."

My mother was a huge fan of history and spent a lot of time dwelling on its consequences. So, our siblings and I had our names decided on those lines. Mutti starred in a role as Joan of Arc in a school play. This was something she was truly proud of. It was performed in a boys' school and she was the only female in the play, and it got rave reviews in German newspapers. And so my sister, Hsiao Hu, was named Joan, for Joan of Arc. My brother Hsiao Pang Tze was now George, after my uncle who had disappeared in his airplane during World War II. And I was Katherine, named after a character in my mother's favorite movie *Henry the V*, which is based on the king who married a French princess named Catherine.

"Where in America are we going to stay?" Hsiao Pang Tze, now George, asked.

Mutti smiled, "We will live with Tante Eva and Onkel Stephan. They are my best friends from Berlin." She explained that in Germany, it was not safe to be Jewish, and Stephan Kuttner's Jewish father had converted to Christianity. Stephan and Eva were in Rome, as Stephan was working for the Vatican, when it became dangerous to be there. Stephan was offered a job in Washington, D.C. as professor of canon law at Catholic

University. He went to Lisbon first and waited for Eva and their three little ones to join him. But it was 1940 and Eva's passport was marked with "JEW." Baba, who was serving as acting ambassador in Italy, offered to help by pretending that Eva was one of his concubines so that she could get a passage to leave, but this did not happen. Instead, it turned out Eva had the help of an escort who lived in the same building as she, whom she befriended when everyone else ignored her. Rumor had it that this kind escort was the daughter of the chief of the secret police, with many important connections. And with their help, Eva was able to join Stephan with her three kids in Lisbon and then the United States.

"They now have seven children," Mutti continued, "We will stay in their basement until I teach myself how to type and try to get a job so we can live in a place of our own."

It was only then that I, now Katherine, realized I had packed all the wrong things. I understood that we wouldn't be returning to China any time soon. Mutti should not have asked me to pack important things, she should have said to pack what I loved best. First I was devastated, then I was angry. Why hadn't she been honest with me? I should have packed my favorite *Max and Moritz* book and the copy of *Little Women* in Chinese that Li Jia Tong had given me for my birthday. He was my best friend. I never wanted to forget him. Could I have been allowed to bring my cat and kittens? Probably not.

Each day on the ship went by much like the last, but one day when I got up and went to breakfast, I noticed that everyone was tense and quiet in the dining room. All morning as I walked around the ship, people had terrified faces—no one spoke. It felt creepy. I was glad to find Joan on the upper deck,

"Why is everyone acting so strangely today? What's going on?" I asked.

"It's Friday the 13."

"So?"

"For many people it is an extremely unlucky day." Joan stretched her arms wide. "Look, our ship is in the middle of the Pacific Ocean; we are miles and miles from any land or other ships! If anything should happen to our ship, there would be no one who could help us."

For the rest of that day, I joined the others in feeling scared. I wished Baba were there. He always comforted me when I was scared. How would he feel if we all drowned? What did he do in the evenings without our company? Is he laughing and smiling less, as we are doing?

I was hesitant to voice my concerns, afraid of offending any spirits and afraid of dying in the middle of the ocean. Thankfully, the day ended with no mishaps.

On May 17, our little family celebrated George's sixth birthday. I had been given a whole dollar of American money before we left China, and it came in handy now. As a surprise, I wrapped a dime with many pieces of paper until the package looked huge. I thought it was a great joke to play on my little brother. When George finally got to the dime after unwrapping so many layers of old newspaper, he smiled. He liked money. Joan gave him her special pen that he had admired, and Mutti gave him a set of toy soldiers she had packed for this special day.

When the ship landed a couple of days later in Hawaii to reload cargo, passengers were allowed to disembark. The ship would be at the harbor for two entire days. Mutti had a school friend from Berlin who lived in Honolulu, and a quick phone call resulted in a lovely invitation for lunch and a swim. Before lunch, Mutti took all of us for a walking tour around the island. The day was breezy. We saw strange, beautiful trees and plants that we had never seen before. Exotic flowers were everywhere.

For me, however, the most astonishing sight was all the people. Most of them looked just like me! In every other place I had ever lived, I didn't fit in. Being Eurasian made me look neither European nor Asian. But here in Hawaii, where so many people were of mixed descent, I looked just like everyone else! It felt wonderful. No one stared at me, trying to figure out what my heritage was.

I wish we were living here, I thought, as we arrived a bit late for lunch at my mother's former classmate's house. Gretchen Schmidt had three kids, Sonia, David, and Andres. They were all teens and begged my sister, who was about their age to join them for a swim after lunch. George and I preferred to play with the toys in their large playroom.

Mutti cautioned Joan to be careful, worrying a bit since my strong-willed sister often disobeyed instructions she thought were silly. The beach stretched endlessly. The water shone with varying hues of blue and green. The four children raced one another, and Joan surprised everyone by consistently winning. She loved challenges. Ultimately, they dared each other to see how far out they could swim. They all took off at once. Joan, a good swimmer, headed out confidently. After what felt like twenty minutes, she felt the current getting stronger, she was getting tired and looked behind her. Sonia and David had stopped but Andres was close behind. She kept going, sure that he would tire soon. After some time, she glanced back and he was smiling behind her, and then she suddenly felt a stabbing pain. A cramp gripped her leg and she doubled up into a ball. She began to sink, and the two teens were too far out in the water for any lifeguard to notice. She cried out and began to slip beneath the surface. Andres was glad he had begun taking lessons three months earlier as a lifeguard trainee. He sped up, grabbed her around her neck, and told her to relax and float facing upwards. For once, she did as she was told and by the time they got to shore, her cramp had eased and she was able to stand and stagger back to the house. All the kids promised not to mention this incident to the adults. Joan swore me to secrecy when she got back, and I have never told anyone until now.

At last, on May 28, 1949, the ship entered the San Francisco harbor. Most of the passengers stood shoulder to shoulder at the bow of the ship, staring at the harbor and the beautiful sight of the Golden Gate Bridge welcoming them. The relief of arriving at our destination after a month-long trip was palpable. I heard excited chatter all around me, but I was fearful. I would no longer understand what people around me were saying, nor could I read what was written. What would our lives be like without servants waiting on us? Mutti has never had a job, would anyone hire her? How would I manage when school began in three months? Mutti jostled me out of my reverie. Joan and I each carried our suitcases, and followed Mutti who was holding her heavy bag in one hand and George's hand in the other. With the other passengers, we all filed down the gangway to the pier, where we each had to present our passports and were thoroughly inspected to ensure that we were not carrying anything illegal, that we had our polio vaccinations, and that all of our documents were in order. It felt queasy walking on land after twenty-four days on a ship.

Once we had cleared immigration, I looked around; there were so many people with pale skin, some with dark skin, some with yellow hair, others with orange hair. It felt weird, coming from what was mostly a homogenous country, to someplace so colorful. Mutti searched the immense crowd for Edna and Victor Frankenhausen, the high school friends from Berlin she had arranged to meet once the ship arrived. We would stay with them in San Francisco for a day, before taking a train to Washington, D.C., our final destination.

"Over here, Barbel!" a voice cried out in the crowd. Mutti looked to her right. There were the Frankenhausens, although she barely recognized them. They all spoke in rapid German as we piled into their car and headed for their home in the suburbs. It had been many years since the three of them had seen one another. The steep hills in the city made me wonder if it'd be fun to race down with Joan.

Our train to Washington, D.C. didn't leave until the afternoon of the thirtieth. So, the next morning, after a restful night without the rocking of the boat, Mr. and Mrs. Frankenhausen decided to take the children for rides at an amusement park. Just before arriving to the park, we stopped at a store. Mutti allowed Joan, George, and me to buy something with the one dollar that we each had. I bought the Sunday newspaper, thick with comics and costing just ten cents. I thought I had found a great bargain.

The amusement park was supposed to be a "Welcome to the USA" treat for us. Joan and George loved all the rides, but I was terrified when the Ferris wheel seat Joan and I were sharing went higher and higher and then began to twirl. Joan laughed happily while I held on with all my might, positive that I would fall out at any second. The roller coaster was even worse. My stomach flew up into my throat. I swore I would never ride either one again.

CHAPTER THREE

The Old Fox at Home

After thanking the Frankenhausens for a lovely visit, our family boarded the train to Chicago, where we had to change trains on our way to Washington, D.C. After two days on the train, we arrived in Chicago at 1:30 p.m., according to Mutti's watch. We had more than five hours before we had to board the other train bound for Washington, D.C., where Tante Eva and Onkel Stephan lived. This gave us enough time to see a bit of Chicago.

We left our luggage at the station's lockers and took off. Chicago looked quite different from San Francisco, although at that point, neither city had homeless people milling in the streets, like in Shanghai. I decided that this must be a good country if they made sure everyone had a home and enough to eat. It surprised me to see a lake in the middle of the city. The elegant buildings in Chicago were less crowded than in San Francisco. We watched the ferry carrying passengers under the bright sky, and visited the Museum of Science and Industry, which had fun interactive displays. George especially liked pushing and pulling their levers to make ships and magnets move. If America had many museums like this one, I thought that I might actually be glad we came. After we left the museum, we planned to stop and find somewhere to eat, when Mutti noticed a large clock on the street, which said 5:35 p.m. She screamed, frantically waving down the first taxi she saw, and pushed us into it, begging the driver to speed us to the train terminal. We sat in silence during the ride, holding our breath–scared to say a single word that might distract the driver. We couldn't afford to miss the train. Luckily, we arrived just minutes before the train pulled out of the station. Mutti realized that she had never reset her watch to Central time, and it still was set two hours earlier to Pacific time. Thank goodness for that street clock!

The next morning our train arrived in Washington, D.C. Tante Eva and Onkel Stephan were right there when our train arrived, beaming as they waited on the platform. Tante Eva hugged each of us. I was not used to hugging and was very uncomfortable standing there, unable to move as she squeezed so tightly and didn't seem to want to let go. Having never been hugged, I hated the feeling and was eager for her to stop.

"Katrinchen, Katrinchen," she repeated the German endearment. "How you've grown. I haven't seen you since you were three!" She seemed so happy to see us. All I wanted to do was to get to where we would live and see if I'd like it there.

Then she hugged Joan, "My goodness how beautiful you are! Your mother tells me you are quite the scholar!" Then she bent down and picked up little George and swung him around.

Everyone was packed into the car and drove to the Kuttner home near the Catholic University where Onkel Stephan worked.

Washington, D.C. was unlike either of the two American cities we were previously in. The National Mall with the Lincoln and Jefferson memorials, the Capitol, and Washington Monument were marvels to behold. But there were no tall buildings like those in San Francisco and Chicago. The flat streets had tracks and overhead cables where streetcars ran, unlike the streetcars in San Francisco that went up and down steep hills. The city's roads looked polished, with no litter. I wondered if street sweepers swept the streets every morning. As we got closer to our destination, the streets were tree lined with pretty houses and small well kept yards in front. I heard my sister Joan read the unfamiliar address, "1600 Otis Street N.E." This would become our home for the foreseeable future. Will I ever like it here? Will this place ever feel like home? How am I going to make friends when I can't speak their language or understand what they say?

The Kuttner family had a large two-story house with an inviting fenced backyard. The house also had a basement for us, the new arrivals, to live in temporarily. Tante Eva also managed to find four beds for our family.

All the Kuttner children were there to greet us when we arrived. Ludwig, the eldest at fourteen, was named after Beethoven. Tante Eva attended many concerts when she was pregnant with him, hoping he'd become musical from hearing beautiful music so early in life. Unfortunately, Ludwig turned out to be the only child in the family with no musical ability, although he tried to learn to play the trombone, with little success. On the other hand, Andrew, aged twelve, was a gifted pianist. Following these two were Susie, nine; Angela, seven; Barbara, five (who was named after my Mutti, Tante Eva's best friend); Tommy, three; and Micky, one.

I was happy to see that Susie was about my age, although I wished I could speak English so we could communicate. Joan's English was already fairly good, as she had been learning it in her boarding school in Shanghai. George learned English easily and became fast friends with Angela.

But it was not as easy for me. I was shy and I struggled to learn. Mutti decided the best way for me to master English was to listen to the radio. Every evening I listened to *Richard Diamond Private Detective* and *The Shadow,* which began every episode with, "Who knows what evil lurks in the hearts of men? The Shadow knows." For weeks it was just noises I heard, and nothing made sense. If anyone said anything to me, I'd stand there mute, feeling embarrassed and stupid.

After a while, some English words slowly began to make sense to me. Mutti borrowed *Winnie the Pooh* for me to try to read. I thought Christopher Robin was a girl. I didn't distinguish "he" and "she," and the illustration of this boy confused me.

One of the few times I smiled was when Susie shared her roller skates with me. The skates were clipped onto the bottoms of our shoes and were tightened with a key. After scraping my knees a few times, I learned to skate up and down the sidewalk and did so with glee.

There was a huge mulberry tree in the field behind the alley at the back of the Kuttner house. I spent hours high up there eating mulberries and looking over to the Franciscan Monastery at the top of the hill. Those were my happy moments when I didn't long to be back home in Shanghai with Baba and friends.

Dinnertime at the Kuttner home was fun with the whole family and us. Milk was delivered in bottles with cream at the very top. Ludwig would hold the bottle and shake the milk so

The Hsu and Kuttner kids

the cream would mix with the rest of the skimmed milk before pouring it out to each child's glass. I was amazed at how strong Ludwig was to be able to shake that heavy glass bottle filled with milk with just one hand!

The Kuttner family usually spoke German to each other at home because it was important for the family to be bilingual. But during the year of our stay with them, the children were asked only to speak English in order to help us learn the language. This was a real gift to the three of us. I have wondered how it impacted young Tommy and Micky who were just learning to speak German at home as well as English, not to hear or learn German for a whole year.

Every afternoon an ice cream truck rang its bell and all the children poured out into the street to greet the truck. Tante

Eva gave the children enough money to buy popsicles, which came in two parts, so each child received half. I saved the wrappers and eventually had enough to mail them in to get a plastic ring complete with a red-eyed skull. It was a magnificent prize. On Sundays, the whole family walked a few blocks over to have dinner with Oma and Opa Illch, the Kuttner children's grandparents. They always prepared a scrumptious dinner for the large family, which now included us. Each child was given a small glass of Pepsi to drink, which I thought was the most delicious thing that I had ever tasted.

Joan and George acclimated to living in the U.S. quite well. However, Mutti was still worried about me and my lack of progress in learning English. I guess she must have noticed that I looked bewildered at times and was not nearly as happy as I had been in Shanghai. I rarely smiled, rarely talked. My face was sullen. I missed crawling into my parents' bed in the mornings, when Baba would scratch my back and ask me about the dream I had, or the books I'd been reading. Mutti recalled that I had loved attending ballet school in Shanghai, and that I was inspired by the movie *The Red Shoes* and had begged for lessons. Mutti reasoned that ballet might help me, the awkward child, become more graceful and enrolled me in a ballet school run by Russian dancers, not far from our home in the French sector of the city. Now, a year later, Mutti thought that once again, ballet school might bring me some happiness, and set off to research ballet schools in downtown Washington, D.C.

Without support from Baba, our financial circumstances were dire. Now, in this new country, with our new life, living in the basement of Mutti's generous friends, Mutti had to beg for a scholarship for me. It was a humiliating experience for Mutti.

I bet she thought, "Here I am, an ex-ambassador's wife, jobless, penniless, and begging for charity." But she was determined to help me adjust to the change. She found a school where the owner agreed to lower the fee for me as long as I was industrious and would come regularly. Mutti and I were delighted! She taught me how to get on the bus, where to transfer to another bus, and finally, where to get off and walk the four blocks to Leon Fokine's School of Ballet near Dupont Circle.

The ballet lessons were just what I needed. I loved every minute of them. One day, after the class ended, a parent told me that I danced well. I was thrilled. No one had ever told me I did anything well. In China, what adults did to encourage children was to tell them they needed to improve. Compliments were given only to the truly exceptional students. This seemingly casual comment not only reinforced my love for dance, but also gave me direction.

I decided then and there that my goal was to become a ballerina. I practiced every day for at least two hours in the basement. Stretching, bending, pointing my toes as I raised my legs. I held my back straight, and forced my feet to point perfectly sideways, like Charlie Chaplin.

One day, while daydreaming on the bus home from ballet class, I missed the stop to transfer. When I realized my error, I got off the bus and tried to retrace the bus route. The more I walked, however, the more lost I became. With my heart racing, I forced myself not to cry, and I continued wandering, looking for any familiar signs. My English was not good enough to ask for directions. I didn't even know the words for "lost" or "bus stop." The day waned and darkness began to fall before I finally found the correct bus stop. I didn't know if my transfer ticket was still good three hours later than I originally planned, but thank goodness the bus driver didn't look to see whether it had expired. I got home to a very worried Mutti, and only then did the tears pour forth.

Soon it was time to start school. My English was still rudimentary. As a result, when people spoke to me, I'd nod my head with a smile and answer, "Yes," to almost anything they said. I was too embarrassed to admit I had no idea what they said or what they wanted. Despite the positive reinforcement in ballet, my confidence overall was at its lowest that year.

When the first day of school arrived, Mutti explained to me how to walk the six blocks down the hill to John Burroughs Elementary School where my brother and I would attend. I was to walk George to his first-grade classroom, bring him home for us to eat lunch, and then walk back to school for our afternoon classes.

It was sunny as George and I made our way to school that first day. As we walked slowly down the hill, the tree lined sidewalks bordering single family homes in Northeast Washington seemed to portend a good day. I held George's small hand, he was beaming in his new sailor suit. I was wearing a new blue dress that Mutti had bought. I had already grown an inch since we arrived in June. Mutti thought it was drinking milk for the first time in years that spurred my quick growth. No one drank milk in China. The only cows we had there were water buffalo, and they were used to plow the fields. At this point Mutti suggested I stop drinking milk as I was growing too fast and she couldn't afford to buy me new clothes every three months.

That first day of school in the U.S. was terrifying. I wasn't sure how to find my sixth-grade classroom, nor how the kids would treat me. Although I was feeling anxious, we walked across the playground area towards the austere, brick school building. I noticed two tall boys walking in my direction. George tried to pull me back, but I dropped his hand.

"Well, looky here! Who is this Chink?" The taller boy walked right over and began to shove me. The other boy laughed out loud. George's eyes grew big as he saw me about to be attacked by these bullies. When the first boy put his hands on my shoulders, I took him by his waist and easily shoved him, along with his shocked buddy, into the rose bushes lining the playground. I guess wrestling with my classmates in China had paid off. As they extricated themselves, with red faces, out of the thorny bushes, the taller boy grumbled, "Better leave this kid alone."

The best was yet to come! A small crowd of children had gathered to watch our arrival to their school and size us up, the newcomers. They all witnessed my success. George smiled with pride and admiration for me, his big sister.

Finally, I found my way to Mrs. Fulgham's sixth-grade class. As I entered the classroom, I bowed to the teacher and to my classmates. The students looked at me and began to laugh. What did I do wrong? Don't children in America bow to each other in the morning? Mrs. Fulgham quieted the class and led me to a desk in the front row. I listened intently to her all day but very little of what she said made any sense. The only time I actually did anything was during arithmetic class when the teacher gave out sheets with problems to solve. The paper had problems using multiplication, division, and fractions, all of which I had mastered in third grade in China. I finished early and felt proud. No one spoke to me, but I was glad since I didn't understand much of anything anyway. I was thrilled that I didn't have to do homework as the teacher realized how little English I understood.

Friday afternoon at 2:30, Mrs. Fulgham announced that the students could choose their favorite songs and sing for the last half hour of school. I sat listening to the unfamiliar songs until suddenly someone chose a song that my teacher in Shanghai had taught us. This was my favorite song. The song narrated traveling down the Swanee River, and I thought it was about foxes, which were my favorite animals. I loved that song because one of the lyrics said, "old folks at home," and I understood it as "old fox at home."

I snapped to attention, so grateful that I was able to sing along with the others.

Every Friday after this, I would raise my hand and request my favorite song about foxes. It would be more than a year before I realized, to my great disappointment, that this song was not only a racist song, but also that it was not about foxes at all. I wondered, "How is it that a song that insults Black people is sung in school? Is there no respect for all peoples in this country? Am I also regarded as inferior by others because I am Chinese?" It was starting to dawn on me that I was always going to feel like a foreigner. In China, I wasn't Chinese enough, but here, I was too Chinese.

By November, my English was getting good enough for me to say a few sentences and understand a little of what was being said. Two classmates, Virginia and Matilda, sometimes invited me to swing with them on the playground during recess. In square dancing classes, Dicky Yowell chose me to be his partner, which made me happy. I wondered if he had a mini crush on me.

One day I complained of a stomachache to Dicky as we danced. "Maybe you are getting your period," he said.

My face flushed. Only last month, Mutti explained about the oncoming changes that may soon occur, and not to be frightened if I found blood in my underpants. "It's called menstruation," she told me.

I pretended not to hear what Dicky said. However, that very evening, I found blood on my underpants and was mortified that Dicky knew better than I about what was happening. How did he know?! Why did I blabber to him that I had a stomachache?!

It was hugely embarrassing for me to attend school the next day. I barely acknowledged Dicky's greeting and his question, "How are you feeling today, Katherine?"

One day, a math test was given, and all the problems were easy except problem number six, which was a word problem. I did not understand the words. So far I had received a one hundred percent positive score on every single arithmetic test. I didn't want to break my record. So I whispered to Dicky, who was sitting next to me, "What is the answer to..." and I held up my fist with my pinky and my thumb raised. Dicky saw my two fingers and whispered the answer for problem number two. It was then that I realized I was using the Chinese sign for six. The Chinese devised a clever way for one hand to show numbers from one to ten,[3] but Dicky obviously didn't know that I showed a six. That was my first and last attempt at cheating. Luckily, Mrs. Fulgham did not count one off for me because she knew I did not

---

[3]The likely reason this was developed was to bridge the gap between the numerous dialects of Chinese.

recognize enough English to be able to solve this question. My perfect record remained intact.

In early December, Mutti allowed me to invite two friends over for my twelfth birthday. Matilda and Virginia came, each carrying a little gift. I was so happy. This was only the second party I had ever had. The first party had been in Shanghai, during third grade, when I was having a horrible time catching up with my classmates in arithmetic after my two years in the rural school in Chongqing. After being tutored every recess by the teacher, I finally got two answers right out of eight problems. It was the first time I'd gotten any problem correct on a math test and Mutti celebrated this great event with a little party for me. There were no gifts there, we ate dim sum and played games in the yard. Here in the U.S. we had cake and ice cream, and I was delighted with my gifts.

Before Christmas arrived that first year in America, there were two major events. First, our visitor's visa was expiring and our family had to leave the country and re-enter, only this time we had to enter as permanent residents, which allowed immigrants to stay as long as they liked with the possibility of becoming citizens if we stayed long enough and passed a test. We flew by plane to Toronto, Canada and stayed with a German doctor Mutti had met in Shanghai. There, this doctor urged Mutti to divorce Baba and marry him instead. He was charming, earned a good living, and was quite good looking. Mutti was flattered, but the doctor was a pathologist, and Mutti didn't want to live with a man who worked on dead people. Our visit to Toronto was our first trip on a commercial plane and very exciting for the four of us. The only other time our family flew on an airplane was when we left Chongqing, and that was on a military transport plane. Instead of individual seats, there were wooden benches on each side of the plane, with blankets for the passengers. The noise was so loud, I could hardly stand it and I put my head on the bench with the blanket on top of my head to muffle the unbearable sound.

The second major event was a hospital trip for George and me to remove our tonsils. Doctors highly recommended this for all youngsters in the 1950s. We were promised as much ice cream as we wanted after the procedure. I was so excited! What disappointment it was to recover from the operation and realize that ice cream did not taste good at all with our throats so sore. The only good thing from that stay was that George and I received two comic books each. We were beyond happy with that.

At the Kuttner home, the four Sundays before Christmas were Advent Sundays. Each Advent Sunday evening, Onkel Stephan would sit at the piano and play Christmas carols. The entire household—all seven Kuttner kids, and we three Hsu kids, along with Eva and Mutti—gathered around the piano and sang. Those evenings were my favorite memories at the Kuttner home; for me, they epitomized what a happy home was.

By the spring, my English had improved somewhat as had my confidence. I no longer nodded blankly as if I understood everything. I even found enough courage to occasionally ask for an explanation when I was confused about the meaning of a word. One day in class, while I was whispering to a friend, Mrs. Fulgham took notice.

"Katherine, you are not only not paying attention to my class, but you are also distracting your classmates. Today you are to stay after school and write a note to your mother." Everyone looked at me. I felt awful. I looked down in shame.

Then I remembered the time I talked in class in Shanghai and was sent out into the hall. I hid in the bathroom so other people would not see me standing outside my classroom. After a half hour, a classmate came knocking on the door to my stall in the bathroom. "You can stop hiding there Hsiao Yu," she said. "Teacher Hsia said you may come back in."

"I am not hiding. I'm peeing," I said, flushing the toilet and hoping she believed my lie.

After all the students had gone home, I sat alone at my desk in Mrs. Fulgham's classroom.

"Go ahead and write that note to your mother," Mrs. Fulgham ordered, "after which you may go home and have her sign it."

I wrote the note in Chinese, knowing full well that although my mother spoke Chinese fluently with barely an accent, she did not learn to read the complicated characters. When I went home, I asked my sister Joan to sign it with Mutti's name. She gladly complied, happy to help me out of a jam.

But I soon found myself in a worse jam that I didn't know how to fix. While attending a ballet class, an elderly gentleman with a camera who had been taking photos of the students for weeks, presented me with a couple of prints that showed me dancing among my classmates.

"Show these to your parents," he said. "My name is Mr. Fawcett and I'd like to take more photos of you. Ask them if you could come to the ballet school on Saturdays to be photographed."

That evening, looking at the photos, Mutti was pleased. Someone finally noticed me, her second daughter. It was usually Joan that everyone admired as she was extraordinarily beautiful, with her curly hair, sparkly eyes, and vivacious personality, or George, the pampered only son with his cute face, bright smile, and outgoing personality. Mutti called the number written on the back of the photos and gave her permission for me to meet him on Saturdays for more photos.

So began the weekly photo sessions. Each week Mr. Fawcett took more photos. He brought tutus and some leotards for me to wear, which were thin and almost transparent. They made me uncomfortable, but all of us children had been taught to obey adults, always. He brought me candy, which I liked. He offered to take me to see a movie. That was such a treat, as I rarely had the opportunity to see a movie. However, during the movie, Mr. Fawcett behaved inappropriately. Back home, I asked Mutti if she could please stop sending me to Mr. Fawcett to have my photos taken.

Mutti was surprised. "I thought you enjoyed having such lovely photos taken for free. He even photographed you at the Freer Gallery with various Chinese artifacts. You said you enjoyed seeing the exhibits, didn't you?"

I looked down and quietly uttered, "I liked the museum and I like the pictures he took of me, Mutti, but I don't like Mr. Fawcett."

"That's fine, I will phone him and cancel next week's photo sessions." I breathed a sigh of relief. It was easier than I thought. If only I had said something sooner.

Much sooner.

If only my Baba were here.

One warm afternoon in May, George and I were walking home from school and on the way home, we saw a neighbor's sprinkler watering his front lawn.

"Let's go under the sprinkler and get wet," George said, "and it will cool us off."

I held on to his hand and replied, "No, Georgie, we will get our clothes wet and dirty. Mutti will be upset with us."

Letting go of my hand, George dashed under the sprinkler anyway, giggling with glee as I stood on the sidewalk, fuming. He never listened to me. When we arrived home, Mutti saw George's sopping clothes and asked what happened to him.

"Katherine pushed me under the neighbor's sprinkler and got me all wet!" he cried. Mutti slapped my face before I had a chance to present my version of the story. George was by far Mutti's most favorite child and was never scolded. Ever. Not even when he played with matches in the Kuttner's backyard and set a fire that almost got out of control. He was invulnerable, and he knew it. We knew it too. Baba, on the other hand, never discriminated amongst us. This was yet again another instance when the distance between us felt so vast. I missed him terribly.

However, I didn't have time to be upset, as Mutti had good news. She finally got a job, even though she was thirty-five years old, with a two-year college degree from Germany, and no job experience whatsoever. The Chinese Military Attaché's Office offered Mutti a job as their secretary. She suspected that they gave her a job as a kindness because many people there knew my Baba. She would need to improve her typing, of course. But her accent was so minimal that many people phoning couldn't tell that she wasn't Chinese. She began work that July.

CHAPTER FOUR

Just Say 'Shoe'

Mutti's job was in Georgetown, so it was time for our family to move closer to her job. She found an adequate apartment, at Kew Gardens on 2700 Q Street N.W., and Tante Eva helped her pack our few possessions. Some of the Kuttner children were sad to lose their playmates, though they had known this was going to happen eventually. Onkel Stephan drove us and our suitcases across the city to the new basement apartment, where the windows faced a well maintained courtyard in the middle of the building. There were benches for residents to enjoy the peace and quiet as they relaxed and viewed the flowering bushes. At the end of the hallway was a laundry room.

Mutti had one bedroom. Joan and I shared the other bedroom, and George slept in the living room on the sofa, where he had to pack up the sheets and blankets each morning and put them in the closet. Joan and I were responsible for sweeping and mopping the floors and washing the dishes. Mutti even learned to cook in the tiny kitchen. Prior to moving to America, she had had two to eight servants for sixteen years. There had been maids to make beds, do laundry, and clean; governesses to raise the children; cooks to prepare meals; and chauffeurs to drive her around. Even at Tante Eva's, Mutti had usually let her friend prepare the meals for the huge family.

Mutti's success in the kitchen surprised even herself. She remembered some delicious German recipes from her youth. She tried various concoctions to replicate the marvelous Chinese dishes we ate in China. She told herself if she could learn five languages, adjust to a totally foreign culture, and learn to type, she surely could learn to cook. Her salary was a meager two hundred dollars a month, so she suggested that I begin to earn some money by babysitting for a neighbor, Jean Battey, who had just had a baby. If I could earn a little money, I could begin to save money to buy my own clothes.

I was excited. I always loved children and the idea of earning fifty cents an hour sounded wonderful. I told the clerk at the apartment office where I stopped to get the mail for the day.

The clerk handed me the letters and bills and said, "Your first babysitting job? A new baby? You'd better not drop him!" That joking remark haunted me for the next two days. I kept thinking of what I'd do if I did drop the baby. I knew I was pretty clumsy.

The night of my first job, I listened carefully to all the directions Mrs. Battey gave me. David, an eight-month-old baby, was already asleep when I got there. I looked in on him several times, hoping he would not wake up, because I really didn't want to pick him up in case I dropped him. Fortunately, he slept soundly. I went home with my first one dollar and fifty cents, absolutely elated.

Living in this new apartment also meant that I could either walk to ballet class or take a bus. It was only about two miles from our apartment, so I could save the ten-cent bus fare if I wasn't too tired to walk home, and it was only a few blocks from George's elementary school.

One day I found an opened letter on the kitchen table that Mutti had forgotten to put away. It was from Baba to Mutti, begging for us to return. I knew it was wrong for me to read her letter, but my curiosity overtook my better judgment. When she returned from work, I asked her why we weren't going back to China to be with him.

"Let me explain, dear," she looked at me with concern, "during the four years when Baba was working with President Chiang Kai-shek, it became harder and harder for Baba because he didn't agree with many of Chiang's policies. Baba was happy when the war ended, so he could quit working with Chiang and get a job in Shanghai as the dean of a law school. But when the Communist government was about to take over the country, many of General Chiang's appointees escaped with him to Taiwan. Baba stayed in Shanghai, because he did not want to be seen as one who agreed with all of Chiang's policies," she said.

She went on, "Soon after the takeover, the Communists forced many officials and other important people to confess their wrongdoings on stage in front of large crowds. Many people were publicly humiliated and beaten, and some were killed. But not your father. Communist officials came to Baba and asked him to join forces with them, but Baba refused. His own father, General Hsu Shuzheng, had worked to oppose the beginnings of the Communist movement in the early 1920s, and for that he was assassinated at age forty-five. Consequently, Baba refused to work for the current Communist government in Shanghai. For that, he was kept under house arrest for an entire year. It only ended when a friend came to visit and sneaked a sailor's uniform to him. Baba grew a beard, and disguised as a sailor, walked out of his home and escaped to Hong Kong."

I was so hopeful. "Oh Mutti, if Baba got to Hong Kong, then he could come straight to us in America!"

"Yes, that is what I thought too," sighed Mutti. "But no, in the United States Baba would be a nobody, whereas in Taiwan he would be admired and revered. He was raised to serve his country. So instead of coming here, he went to Taiwan, and is begging me to join him with all of you."

"Let's go!" I jumped up.

"No, dear, the island of Taiwan is so overcrowded with refugees from the mainland after the civil war, that only one child out of seven can pass the stringent exam to enter school. It's no place to raise children. All three of you would get a better education in the United States. I have urged Baba to come join us but that presents a problem. He has published many articles in the newspaper against President Chiang, infuriating him, and since Taiwan needs military support from the United States, Chiang does not want Baba coming here and badmouthing him. So Baba is now unable to leave and might be put under house arrest there."

I couldn't believe what Mutti just told me—I had so many questions. I had broken countless wishbones from chickens in the hope that Baba would soon join us, and now I am told that he chooses to serve his country rather than come to be with us. Didn't he love us? I knew he had begged Mutti to bring us back to Taiwan, but that Mutti had declined. Had she stopped loving him because he chose not to come with us in the first place? Mutti says we need to stay in the U.S. for the best education—that if we went back, only the top scorers would be accepted in schools. Which meant Joan and George, who consistently scored over the ninetieth percentile, and not me; I would panic before and during exams and rarely score well. So this is why Mutti calls me stupid occasionally? Is it because of me that we are not returning to be with Baba?

I spent the rest of the summer missing Baba, wishing that somehow, he would be allowed to leave Taiwan and join us.

Finally, September came and I was to begin junior high school at Gordon Junior High. I thought to myself, "I wonder

Katherine, pictured in the center of the middle row, with her Gordon Junior High classmates

if I'll do okay there?" The day before school started, all the new students had to go in for a day of testing to determine the section into which they would be placed. Although my vocabulary in English had improved in the last year, I realized that I didn't understand a fair amount of the questions on the test. The children who tested well were placed in 7A1. The children who missed a number of questions were placed in 7A2. Those who missed many questions were in 7A3. I found myself assigned to 7A2, along with several children of embassy personnel, immigrants, and some refugees. They were Maija from Latvia; Carlos, grandson of the archbishop of Sweden; and Lydia from Bolivia. All four of us had been in the U.S. a short time and were still learning English.

On the first morning of school, a young new teacher with an elegant gray suit, a starched white shirt, and a blue silk tie walked into our classroom. He wrote his name on the blackboard, in all capitals: MR. LANDIS.

Smiling, he said, "That's my name, children. This is my first day teaching. Please sit down."

Almost all of the students stood up, but I sat down, obediently. When I saw all my classmates defy the new teacher, I joined them by standing up. For once, I had purposely acted badly, and it was truly one of the most joyous moments in my life! I felt powerful for the first time. Mr. Landis stood there wordlessly, not knowing how to act. We all broke out in laughter, even Mr. Landis, who asked us once more to sit down. We complied.

He called the roll. When he got to my last name, Hsu, he didn't know how to pronounce it and asked me. I said, "It is pronounced 'Shu,' like the French U or the German U sound. Most Americans can't say that sound so you can just say 'Shoe,' which is okay." I knew everyone had trouble with my last name; they didn't know what to do with the initial letter H. Some people pronounced my name as "Huh Soo" and I accepted that because it felt useless to correct them.

As I entered school on the third day, I saw some classmates sitting on the wall, which bordered the school playground.

"Hi, Katherine Shit," the boys called out.

"Hi," I replied, happy that my classmates were trying to pronounce my last name correctly. The boys laughed, and I laughed too, thinking they were trying so hard. Every morning for the next few weeks the boys all happily greeted me with "Katherine Shit" and I happily greeted them back. When Maija finally heard it and told me what it meant, I was mortified. The next morning I tried a different route to enter the school in order to avoid those horrid boys, but during recess they taunted me, repeating their nasty name calling over and over, laughing all the while.

When I got home that afternoon, I looked in the bathroom mirror at the shape of my slanted eyes. "If only my eyes were round like everyone else's in my class, no one would tease me," I thought. So I pulled and stretched my eyes this way and that without success. They just snapped back to the original slanted shape. I was ugly and there was nothing I could do about it. Walking out of the bathroom, I slammed the door. Some of my anger dissipated with the sound of the door slamming, though I still felt angry. Angry at the bullies at school, angry at looking different, angry about not being accepted.

"Whoa," I thought to myself, "I am having a temper tantrum. My parents had named me Little Jade, hoping I would be poised, calm and gentle, in control of my emotions.... Hmmm."

I got out my violin, as it usually made me happy to practice with it. I put it under my chin, bowing it. The screeches were improving, and in a short time, I forgot about being angry. Instead I thought about how lucky I was that Mutti allowed me to take free violin lessons at school.

When I'd first broached the idea of violin lessons to Mutti, she had refused. "Absolutely not, Katherine. Your grandmother's occupation was teaching violin lessons. Every day coming home from school, I heard her students play. Beginners sound dreadful. It takes years before anyone can get lovely sounds from the instrument. I simply can't stand the idea of having to listen to screeching every evening when I come home from work. Just forget this idea right now," she said.

I cried. For three whole evenings I implored Mutti to let me take the lessons, only to hear, "No."

Finally, on the third night, Mutti said, "If you promise NEVER to practice when I am home, I will sign your permission slip to rent the school violin and to take free lessons."

"Yes!" I was elated. The two things that made me happiest in my childhood were taking dance lessons and practicing my violin, which I did every afternoon after school.

That winter, my ballet school was presenting a recital at the Lisner Auditorium on the campus of George Washington University. The best dancers had the solo parts in *The Nutcracker*, and the other students did group dances. My class practiced an Asian dance, which ended with all sixteen of us jumping up and down eleven times with pointer fingers up, then landing in a seated position, cross-legged, on the twelfth beat.

On the afternoon of the dress rehearsal, we were all thrilled to be wearing fancy costumes on a huge stage. Tickets were sold to see us perform that evening. I was so excited that after jumping ten times, I sat down as the rest of the "Asian" dancers jumped one more time and landed a beat after me. I was embarrassed when I exited backstage, and Mr. Fokine was livid.

"How is it that you can't count, Kati! What's wrong with you?! We practiced this dance a million times," he hollered.

That night, in the real performance, I was petrified. I assured myself that I wouldn't mess up this time. I thought he would kill me, or I would kill myself. I was so nervous I didn't eat supper before leaving for the theater. When it was our turn to perform, Mr. Fokine looked at me threateningly, "Do it right!" I did all the steps correctly, all the way to the end. As I began the twelve jumps, I heard Mr. Fokine counting aloud backstage, "ONE, TWO, THREE, FOUR... TWELVE." All of the Asian dancers landed sitting down. All except me. I jumped a thirteenth time. I was so focused on not landing too early that I ended up landing late instead. The audience laughed. Good thing Mutti didn't come. Mr. Fokine didn't speak to me for weeks.

I played and replayed the scene in my mind, feeling shame all over again. I thought nothing could make me feel that badly ever again, but I was wrong. One evening, as I was about to leave for a babysitting job, Mutti told me that she and Baba were going to get a divorce. He was not able to get permission to leave his country and Mutti did not want to return. We three were getting a good education here in the U.S. and it was too difficult to continue being married so far from each other.

I was devastated. I adored my father. With him I felt loved. His sense of humor made me smile. I hadn't laughed much since we left him. This news made me want to scream, to cry, to argue, but I was already five minutes late for my babysitting job. I also wanted to live up to my given name by controlling my emotions and staying calm. So I left for my job, and kept my feelings bottled up; it was unbearably painful. I hadn't seen Baba in two years. Did he regret his decision not to join us? A couple of years later, he married one of his young students at the university, Nancy.

My friendship with Maija provided some comfort. When we whispered to one another in class, I was usually the one who was scolded, so Maija decided we should learn Morse code and write notes instead. For a while that worked well; we passed notes regularly until one day when the geography teacher intercepted one. As the note was being passed from one student to the next on its way from me to Maija, the teacher grabbed it triumphantly. She smiled as she opened it, but her smile disappeared when she saw the message was written in code.

This geography class was taught by a mean-spirited teacher, who none of the students liked. She treated her students with disdain, mocking us when we made mistakes.

One day someone suggested an idea, "How about all of us remain totally silent in class today? No one raises their hand? No one speaks. We all just sit!"

Everybody agreed. We thought the idea was hilarious. The teacher became angrier and angrier, as she continued asking questions that no one answered. When she called on students, no one moved. It was as if she were teaching a group of statues.

The class was delighted, thinking that we had pulled off a fast one. We laughed ourselves silly for days afterward. We realized that we had power and it felt exhilarating; until report time arrived and every single one of us received an F. She retaliated in her usual manner. She taught us who was in charge. Some of the students knew their parents were going to be extremely upset with an F on their report card. Luckily for me, Mutti never bothered about grades. She knew the changes to a different country, language, and culture would take time. Maybe she never expected me to excel in school. Or, she might have been too wrapped up with her job and the stress of raising a young family with no servants to help her.

In mid-January, the city had its first snowstorm of the year. I arrived at school bundled up in my winter coat. As I walked up to the building, the same nasty boys from before grabbed me. Two of them held me as the third stuffed snow inside the back of my coat, jamming one handful after another until my entire coat was packed with snow, then they let me go, laughing at their antics, calling out, "Chink Chink Chinaman."

I held my tears. I would not give them the satisfaction of seeing me cry. Instead, I walked away from them, took off my coat, and shook it until most of the packed snow fell. I then walked inside the school and to my locker, holding the coat as it continued to drip snow in the hallway. One day I will be famous, I said to myself, then they will be sorry they were so nasty to me.

Winter was brutal, but spring brought with it new experiences. The cherry blossom trees around the National Mall in Washington came out in full bloom—and, as was, and still is, tradition, a cherry blossom festival was held. That year my ballet class was performing a Japanese themed ballet for the festival. We practiced hard and I made an effort to learn each step in order to not upset Mr. Fokine again.

The big draw that spring was the Teen Idol, Eddie Fisher, (later to become the father of Carrie Fisher, Princess Leia of *Star Wars* fame), who was to sing. I brought my fishing pole and a couple of earthworms I dug up. I thought I might catch a fish in the Tidal Basin while waiting for our turn to perform. I cast my line and the hook snagged another dancer behind me. Luckily, it only caught her costume. I decided to give up trying to fish.

When Eddie Fisher arrived, all the girls gathered around him and asked for a photo to be taken with him. I had heard him singing "Oh! My Papa" on the radio, but I didn't realize who this cute young man was. When I came to have my photo taken by my friend, Eddie Fisher put his arm around me, shocking me. No boy had ever done that! And a stranger to boot! To this day, this is one of my favorite snapshots.

That summer, our little family enjoyed swimming in the neighborhood pool. Mutti met a man named Henri Noel there, and they quickly became friends. Both spoke French fluently. Henri had grown up in France as the son of a United Press International correspondent. After he received his PhD in Paris, he joined the army and learned Japanese, and was sent to Japan as a spy during World War II.

Afterwards, he worked as a bibliographer at the Library of Congress. When Mutti found a nicer apartment across the street from Dumbarton Oaks in Georgetown, Henri helped her quietly move the night of August 31 without giving advance notice to the managers at Kew Gardens. They hoped this trick would keep her from having to pay the September rent in our old apartment.

It worked. Mutti knew it wasn't honest, but money was so tight and paying rent in advance at the new apartment made this sneaky move necessary. She had paid the managers of her old apartment her August rent in full and had left it in sparkling condition. Mutti's two-hundred-dollar monthly salary needed to be budgeted carefully to support the four of us. Groceries, for example, were chosen by what was on sale. When my classmate bought a ham sandwich for lunch, I envied her wealth and wished that I could do the same. I often opted to walk home from my ballet classes at 11 p.m. in order to save a dime for the bus fare. My teeth were in bad shape and Mutti sent me to Georgetown Dental School where prices fit our budget. I had many cavities and root canals done. Novocaine would cost an extra seventy-five cents, so I declined the anesthesia. As the drill bore deeper and deeper into my teeth close to the root, instead of screaming in pain, I gripped the arms of the dental chair with all my might, saying to myself, "Mutti needs that seventy-five cents, Mutti needs the money." Since I had a December birthday, I would receive one gift that represented a Christmas and birthday gift, which made me feel quite unlucky not to have been born in March or May, as my siblings had been. Once in a while, Mutti would give George a dime for a comic book or a popsicle. I felt this was quite unfair since I never got anything extra, forgetting completely about the violin lessons she was paying for. However, she did give us fifty cents a week for our allowance. I remember when I was angry at George and deliberately wrecked his Slinky toy, Mutti made me pay for a new one with three weeks of my allowance.

The new apartment on the third floor in a row of apartments was much nicer and cost less. Across the street was a cemetery, where George would sneakily take the fresh flowers left there and bring them home for Mutti. Next to the cemetery was the recreation center with a large field for games, and next to the recreation center were the beautiful gardens of Dumbarton Oaks, a sprawling public park with terraced gardens and vistas, orchards, kitchen gardens, and a vast wilderness of meadows and wooded pathways, as well as a museum.

There was also an unused swimming pool, but a large fence prevented people from entering except by the official entrance. Our family found another entrance along the edge of the park, which turned out to be a great place to hide Easter eggs on Easter Sunday. While there were large signs displayed that said, "THIRTY DOLLAR FINE FOR PICKING FLOWERS," Mutti would pick a bouquet and bring them home saying, "Look, I got some thirty-dollar flowers for us."

Joan and George thought it was a great joke, but I didn't like the idea of dishonesty. Maybe my desire to be honest came from my new interest in religion. None of us children had been baptized. My Chinese Baba didn't care about religion. Mutti was raised in a heavy duty Lutheran atmosphere in Berlin and wanted to spare her children that oppressive religious upbringing. Instead, we were told we could choose a religion someday.

I had become friends with a classmate, Cecile Anschutz, a daughter of an Episcopalian minister at Christ Church Georgetown. She suggested I join a teen group that met every Saturday evening at the church for games and fun, along with some religious instruction. I loved those gatherings and began to develop a bit of a crush on the new deacon, G. Harris Collingwood, a recent graduate of St. John's College and a seminarian. Soon I decided to become baptized and on St. Andrew's Eve, with Tante Eva and my family in attendance, I was baptized. I could choose to have a middle name, and I chose "Elizabeth." After this, I began to read the Bible daily, and often argued with my classmates about its contents. I kept running to Harris when I couldn't defend myself. I didn't realize that Catholics and Protestants used different versions of the Bible. I wasn't well versed in the Christian religion just yet, and poor

Harris made me promise NOT to discuss religion with anyone for two years.

That summer, the church sent me for a two-week conference on racial prejudice that took place in Grand Rapids, Michigan. I was happy to be chosen for this adventure. We congregated in a large auditorium, around five hundred youngsters from all around the United States. The big event was one afternoon. Ralph Bunche, an extraordinarily brilliant African-American who taught at Harvard (and who later became the first Black American to win the Nobel Peace Prize), came to lecture us about the insidiousness of racism. Since I was the only person of color among the five hundred participants, for the remainder of the conference, everyone treated me like a queen. All the kids wanted to make sure they were not seen as prejudiced. One boy, Ray Becker, who lived in Grand Rapids, took me for rides in his Corvette. We continued our friendship by mail for years. I named my parakeet after Ray, and I have loved Corvettes ever since.

CHAPTER FIVE

Dance Class

That fall, Joan left for Bennington College at the tender age of sixteen with a full scholarship. When she first came to the U.S., the high school asked her how old she was, so they'd know what grade to place her in. Joan was fourteen, according to how the U.S. determined age, but she told the school she was sixteen, because in China, a child is considered one year old as soon as he/she is born and on New Year's Day everyone is one year older. The school, therefore, placed her in the eleventh grade. Additionally, because she was quick to learn, she excelled, graduated from high school, and was happy as a lark to attend college in Vermont with a full scholarship.

While Joan attended college, George walked to the elementary school on his own three blocks away, and I took the bus to Gordon Junior High to begin eighth grade. By now I had made friends, and the year began smoothly. I had practiced my violin all summer, so the music teacher was delighted and put me in the orchestra immediately. In my new class, I noticed a tall handsome boy named Glen. I hoped to get his attention but he never seemed to notice me at all. I tried bumping into him as we walked to classes in the hallway, knocking over the books he carried. He looked at me with annoyance, which was not my intended result! So the next couple of days, I wadded up short strips of paper, bent them in half, and shot little missiles with a rubber band at him, across the aisle, hitting him in the arms and legs. He only shot angry faces in return. I obviously wasn't good at flirting, and all these attempts flopped. At last I gave up and decided that he just didn't like me.

Two weeks later, Davi, a classmate from Finland asked me whether I had seen the movie *The Red Shoes*, and said it was playing at the movie theater that week.

"Oh, yes," I smiled, "I saw it in Shanghai. It's a wonderful movie, you should go see it." It only occurred to me later that Davi was about to ask me on a date. This would have been my first date, if only I had answered his question differently. I came to regret answering so quickly without thinking first. However, my English was becoming more fluent, and I was doing well in all my classes except Home Economics.

My Home Economics teacher took an immediate disliking to me. Whatever I did in my sewing class, she berated me loudly and vehemently, pointing out how crooked my stitches were, how poorly I cut the fabric, how my seams didn't match, or how I didn't align the pattern on the bias. The teacher seemed so patient with my classmates, but I could do nothing right. Those hours in the classroom were so painful for me that I decided never to sew. I told myself that it was a skill that I simply could not master. Lo and behold, ten years later as a mother, to save money, I sewed all my children's clothes, as well as my husband's shirts.

Arithmetic classes on the other hand continued to be a breeze. Whatever was asked of the students, I already had done in fifth grade in China. Every single paper was marked with one hundred percent. I was admired for this. I could barely believe it since it had been my worst subject in China. Strangely, my early math aptitude proved to be a problem when the counselors asked me at the end of the year whether I planned to take Extensive or Intensive classes in high school.

I had no idea what that meant. They explained that children who planned to go to college took Intensive classes, and everybody else took Extensive classes. Mutti had told me several times that I wasn't as smart as my siblings. I didn't know if this was her way of making me work harder in school, but I truly believed I wasn't smart. The school counselor said that because I had learned all my math in China and received perfect scores on all my assignments in junior high, there was no need to take a single math class in high school. So I didn't. It sounded fine to me because I planned to become a dancer after high school. Dancing continued to be my main obsession. I had begun to dance with toe shoes three months earlier. My toes still bled as I danced, the bloody lamb's wool within the shoes had to be tossed after each class, but gradually my toes were becoming calloused and bled less often. My immediate goal was to be chosen to be a part of the "company." The company comprised the dancers chosen by Leon Fokine to perform ballets such as *Swan Lake, Les Sylphides,* and *The Nutcracker*. His practice was to brand his chosen girls by piercing their ears, and so on my fifteenth birthday in December, Mr. Fokine walked into my class handing me a small ribboned box and said, "happy birthday, Kati!"

I was surprised and delighted, until I opened it to find a pair of earrings. He then produced a needle and an ice cube. He rubbed the ice cube on my earlobe as my classmates watched. I knew my mother would be horrified if I had pierced ears. She thought pierced ears were ugly and vulgar, but I didn't dare say no to the teacher I was so anxious to please. After icing my earlobe, he stuck the needle in and immediately inserted the new earring. He repeated this on my other ear as my classmates clapped. Although I feared my mother's reaction, I thought that perhaps this was the prelude to an invitation to join the company and learn the real ballets.

Mutti was upset about my ears when I arrived home, but I lied and told her how pretty I felt with the earrings on and how happy they made me. Mutti was angry that Mr. Fokine pierced my ears without consulting her. She might have thought about complaining, but because I was on scholarship, she didn't want to jeopardize that. Eventually she stopped being angry. Maybe she decided the earrings looked nice on me. And after a while, I got used to them and felt they made me prettier.

I started to work extra hard, hoping to be asked to join the elite company. Five months later in early May, Mr. Fokine told me I had been chosen. My first rehearsal was to be the following Saturday at 2 p.m. It was one of the happiest days in my young life. I skipped and ran all the way home. Nothing had ever made me so happy.

That Saturday morning was a warm, gorgeous day, as I set out my ballet gear: leotard, tights, toe shoes, ballet slippers, and rubber leg wrappers, which I hated. My mother had insisted I wear them under my tights whenever I danced because when Mutti was a teen in Berlin, she babysat for Marlene Dietrich, the world famous German movie star. While looking after Marlene's baby, she learned about the rubber leg wrappers that made Marlene's legs so beautiful.

Just before I was about to leave for my first rehearsal, Mutti reminded me it was George's ninth birthday and because the weather was so perfect, we were all going with Henri to the beach for a picnic celebration.

"No, Mutti, I can't, I really can't. I have my first rehearsal for the company. I can't miss it."

"That's ridiculous. Today is George's birthday. Call Mr. Fokine and explain that you are going on a family picnic and you will go to the next rehearsal," Mutti insisted.

Ballet became Katherine's joy.

I had no choice. I called and explained. When I went to my next class, Mr. Fokine told me that I'd lost my place in the company. I sobbed, sobbed, and begged to be reinstated. It was not to be.

Later, when Mutti realized that the trip to the beach had cost me my greatest wish, she found a summer dance camp held in Sedgwick, Maine. Running the camp were two modern dance instructors, both former dancers who had a studio on Wisconsin Avenue in Georgetown. One teacher, Evelyn De La Tour, had danced with Merce Cunningham and Ruth St. Denis. Her partner, Pola Nirenska, had studied with Mary Wigman in Germany. Mutti negotiated a scholarship for me to attend the camp.

When I arrived in Maine in early June for my two months of dance, I was transformed. Shoes were not worn, positions in modern dance were fluid; this was a freedom I had never felt in my ballet classes. Since I was neither a beginner nor advanced in modern dance, I attended the beginner class at 9 a.m., the intermediate class at 10 a.m., and the advanced class at 11 a.m. After lunch I attended three more classes. I loved dancing six hours a day. The seventh class, held once a week, was a composition class, which I needed, since choreographing dances was hard for me. All twenty of the camp dancers slept in a large dorm with beds next to one another.

My job as a scholarship student was to sweep the upstairs dance studio every morning before classes began, along with Hildy Smith, another scholarship student. Before sweeping the studio, Hildy and I first shook out the spread that covered the piano. As we leaned out the window shaking the huge cover together, we joked that a handsome knight on horseback would come riding up the road and rescue us from this tower of torture. We became the best of friends. I even convinced Hildy to transfer to my school the following year so that she, and our other good dance friend, Karen Wentworth, could all be together in the same high school.

Karen was an only child with eccentric parents who held weekly music sessions at their home dance studio. Their friend Mike Seeger, brother of the famous folk singer Pete Seeger, came every Friday night. Mike was drafted into the army, but he registered as a conscientious objector and refused to go to war. In 1952, no one respected that brave decision. He was generally despised as a coward and forced to work in a veterans' hospital cleaning toilets and doing whatever other unpleasant jobs they could find for him. But Mike loved coming to the Wentworth home every Friday night to play his fiddle or his mandolin, and that was where I learned all the Seeger folk songs. Mike taught me how to play the mandolin and how to square dance, and most of the time when he played, we sang with him. Other times, he played while Karen, Hildy, and I danced to the music in the spacious studio. Secretly, I had quite a crush on Mike with his beautiful dark hair that fell over his dark eyes as he played his fiddle. He had a melodious voice and gentle manner. Those Friday nights were some of the happiest times of my teen years.

As a dance student, I became extremely close to Ms. Nirenska. She complimented and encouraged me regularly, assuring me that my future as a professional dancer was highly plausible. For the next couple of years, she became my guide and mentor. At the end of the summer, she managed to get me a full scholarship at all of the major modern dance studios in D.C., where I spent every afternoon dancing, after I finished school for the day. I didn't put forth much effort doing schoolwork, having decided that I was too stupid to attend college; instead, I focused my energy on doing my best in dance.

During that summer in Maine, we were taken to swim in the lakes. I thought God must have placed ice in the lakes because I had never felt so cold. But I had to admit that after the initial shock of the freezing water, it felt good. Occasionally, a weed clung to one of my legs. Every time, I was certain it was a snake and would startle.

One day that summer, some important guests of the teachers watched a performance. Afterwards, we were all introduced to the dignitaries, who had lunch with us. One man told me he worked for the State Department. When I told him how much I missed my father who was not permitted to leave Taiwan because he had become critical of Chiang Kai-shek's policies, this man told me he had the means to help get my father out. He promised to look into it. I was thrilled to hear that and prayed hard for him to succeed in bringing my Baba to the U.S. to join us.

Two months later in October, Mutti went on a weekend trip with Henri, her beloved companion, when this State Department official gave me a call. It was about 9:30 p.m. when the phone rang. George and I were about to get ready for bed. The official said that he called because he had really good news about my father and he'd like to come and talk to me about it, and he needed my address.

I gave him my address because I was so excited about the possibility of seeing my father again. But as soon as I hung up, I began to regret having given it to him. It was very late and I was worried. George and I were home alone, and Mutti had cautioned me never to have a man in our house without her there. What was I to do?

I told George someone might be coming over because I had mistakenly given him our address, and that I would not answer the door when the man arrived. We made sure our door was locked and we scrunched down in the farthest room from the door and waited, hiding under a blanket. Before long, we heard the sound of someone climbing up the outside steps. Then a knock on the door. We held our breath. More knocks. We didn't move.

The man began to shout, "Open the door, Katherine!" and continued to bang and bang on the door. Our hearts were beating almost as loudly as the pounding on the door, but we didn't move. After an interminably long time, we heard retreating steps.

On Monday when I went to the dance studio, Ms. Nirenska was furious. She had evidently given the man my phone number when he had requested it at her dinner party. She then overheard his phone call and noticed him writing down my address. "Why did you invite him, drunk, to come to your house so late at night?!" she asked.

I explained that I thought he had news to give me about my father, and as soon as I gave him my address, I regretted it and never opened the door. Ms. Nirenska was relieved to hear the outcome.

The next day, Mutti returned relaxed and glowing from her trip with Henri. I was growing jealous of the attention she gave to this man who I saw as an intruder. Who was he to take away our mother's attention? I talked about this with Deacon Harris at Christ Church. He asked, "Do you love your mother?"

"Yes, of course I do," I answered.

"This man makes your mother happy, Katherine."

I hadn't thought of that. Harris gave good advice. When I complained that George was too spoiled, and not ever nice to me, he suggested that I go out of my way to treat George with love and kindness. I tried that by going out and spending my whole allowance on a little gift for George. I was shocked the following week when George bought me a surprise gift. It made me so happy, I decided to take the two of us for a real treat. The next Saturday, we took several street cars to go to a theater that was over an hour away to watch *Count of Monte Cristo* and thirty-two cartoons, which included characters like Bugs Bunny and Elmer Fudd, Mr. Magoo, Donald Duck and Scrooge McDuck, Sylvester the Cat, Tweety Bird, and Yogi Bear! For the cost of one ticket, we were entertained for three-and-a-half hours. It was an incredibly fun afternoon for both of us.

It seemed as if Mutti and Henri talked about me during their trip, because when they returned, Mutti suggested that I take lessons in Chinese from a colleague of hers at the Military Attaché's Office. It was true that I was beginning to forget how to read Chinese characters. My vocabulary was okay because Joan and I gathered with a group of young Chinese students regularly. Sometimes we attended dances, sometimes the group held picnics, and other times we performed plays. A new play had been written and I was given the main role. However, I kept stumbling over the words that I couldn't read. In Chinese, there isn't an alphabet to sound words out. Each word looks different and has to be memorized. There are 50,000 characters. One needs to know about 3,000 to read a newspaper, and many students in fifth or sixth grade haven't yet memorized enough to read a newspaper.

The playwright finally gave my part to another girl whose reading vocabulary was much better than mine. However, in May 1952, I was asked to perform a walk-on part, playing the wife of a Chinese ambassador in a play called First Lady, to be performed in the Gayety Theater in D.C. starring the famous actress Helen Gahagan. I had to get a social security number because I would be paid. I left after my walk-on part and did not stay for nightly curtain calls, because then I'd have to catch the bus at 11 p.m. and would be too tired for school the next day. One night, there were all sorts of strange men hanging around backstage.

"What's happening? What are these men doing here?" I asked an actor.

"Didn't you hear? President Truman is attending the show tonight because Helen Gahagan Douglas campaigned to be a senator from California."

I was excited to be performing in front of the President. Unfortunately, I missed the best part. Had I stayed for the curtain call that night, my castmates told me that I'd have been able to shake President Truman's hand, as he greeted everyone backstage after the show!

There was no question that weekly Chinese lessons would be helpful to me. A young Lieutenant Li had arrived from Taiwan recently to work at the Chinese Military Attaché's Office. He seemed to be a pleasant fellow and eager to learn about this country and what young men do in America. So every Thursday evening, I gave up going to dance classes, and instead, Lieutenant Li and I spent a couple of hours reading and speaking Chinese. The beautiful language was coming back. A couple of months later, Lieutenant Li asked if I would like to go bowling with him on Saturday night. I had never been bowling and neither had he. That night, I had a great time because I scored higher than Lieutenant Li. As someone who'd typically felt inferior, I enjoyed competition, especially winning. Mutti told me later that on Monday, Lieutenant Li came in to work in a foul mood, and spent every evening after work that week at the bowling alley. The next Saturday, he invited me to bowl again, and he performed much better than I did. A month or two later, Lieutenant Li asked for my hand in marriage. It made no sense to me since I was fifteen years old and thought of him as my teacher. Mutti immediately put a stop to the weekly lessons.

At school, I told this story to Carlos, the Swedish boy I had befriended.

"I'm ugly and stupid, Carlos," I said. "Why would Lieutenant Li want to marry me?"

"You're neither ugly nor stupid, Katherine," Carlos responded. "You are just fine the way you are. You could get any boy's attention that you wanted. I promise you!"

"You are teasing me."

"Look, Katherine," he continued, "we are both invited to Amy's party next Saturday, right? When we are there, look over all the boys and tell me who you wish would take you out on a date and I'll make sure it happens." I laughed. Carlos was so sweet. I agreed to play along. That afternoon I went to Hildy's house. She had all sorts of beautiful dresses, which she let me borrow. She even gave me some. We chose a spectacular dress for me to wear to Amy's party.

That Saturday night, I walked to Amy's house, about eight blocks away from mine in Georgetown. It was crowded with lots of people I didn't know. Carlos was there, urging me to pick the young man I'd like as a possible date. As I walked around looking, I saw Hans Morsbach, a tall, broad-shouldered, very handsome young German man who had come to the party with Sarah, his date. I told Carlos, "That one," and I pointed to Hans.

"Okay, this is what you are to do, Katherine," he whispered. "When he happens to be alone, I will engage him in a conversation, you wait about three minutes into our chat and then come up to us. I will introduce you, and back out. You then talk, smile, flirt, and see what happens. He will fall for you, I promise."

I did exactly as Carlos directed. He told me I could win over any boy. Really? Okay, this was a test. Hans and I ended up talking and dancing all evening. He took me home that night and ditched Sarah. I should have felt bad for her, but I didn't. I couldn't believe that what Carlos said was true, that I was a fine person and people would like me just the way I am. That advice changed my horrible self-image and gave me a confidence I'd never had before. It wasn't so much that I craved boys' attention. What I needed to learn was to accept myself. I needed to decide I was okay. I needed to learn to like myself, to forgive my flaws and dumb decisions. Instead of struggling to gain approval everywhere, I should just do the best I could with what I had.

When the school year was about to end, Maija told me that her family had found a nice apartment on the other side of town. They planned to move, and she would attend another school the following year. I was devastated. Maija had been my best friend for two years: supporting me when I felt discouraged, and laughing with me when we got away with being a bit naughty in class. I told Maija, "Listen, my sister Joan keeps saying how badly she feels about having lost touch with all her friends in China. Promise me that you and I will stay friends always."

"That's a good idea," Maija responded, "Let's plan to meet at the National Gallery of Art once a month on the weekend." That was our plan in May 1952, which we executed without fail. We continued our friendship with letters throughout our lives, finally meeting in person again in May 1989, when Maija was a professor of physiology at Cornell University, when my middle daughter received her PhD there.

CHAPTER SIX

Extensive, Intensive?

Eighth grade finished well enough. My violin playing had improved during my two years of instruction and dedicated practice. In fact, Mutti came home early from work one day and overheard me playing. She was surprised by the progress I'd made. "Katrinchen! I can't believe it. You are playing pretty well."

"My orchestra teacher said the same thing; he made me the first violinist in our orchestra, and concertmistress," I said proudly.

Mutti said, "I am pleased to discover you might be talented in violin playing like your grandmother. I am going to find you a good teacher so you can hone your skills." She set me up with a German violin teacher. He was strict, and made me practice scales. It wasn't fun. Mutti routinely asked if I had practiced and that changed my attitude completely. I used to love practicing every single day, because I was doing it for myself. But now that Mutti was spending her hard-earned money on my lessons, practicing became something I needed to do for her, and it took all the joy out of it for me. I hated playing scales. I wanted to play melodies. After a year, I switched to an American teacher who allowed me to play whatever I chose.

That summer I revisited the dance camp in Maine. Ms. De La Tour and Ms. Nirenska gave me such encouragement and support that when I returned home at the end of the summer, I decided to quit my ballet lessons altogether and attend only modern dance classes. Ballet offered very strict movements whereas modern dance allowed dancers to express themselves. In modern dance, I found the freedom that I had been missing and longed for in dance.

We went back to school again at the end of the summer, and I began as a freshman at Western High School. On the first day, all one hundred of us freshmen jammed into the auditorium for an introduction from the assistant principal. He told us the rules, and then told us that in addition to academics, the boys would have classes in woodworking and the girls would have classes in home economics. I raised my hand.

"Why can't girls take woodworking?" I don't remember the assistant principal's answer, but I do remember that it caused everyone to laugh. When I got my schedule the next day, I discovered that I had been the only girl assigned to woodworking.

It turned out to be one of the most interesting and enjoyable classes that I had in high school. The teacher told me how different it was to have a girl in his class. He said that normally the boys cursed regularly during the class as they made spice racks and wooden games. But in my class, not only did the boys not use foul language, several were ready to help me whenever I had trouble.

That first month, the drama club was auditioning actors for *A Midsummer Night's Dream*. I tried out for the part of Puck, a mischievous sprite. When the Drama Club members gathered to vote for who played which part, most of them chose me to play Puck. But the dissent was strong. "She's a freshman! She has to wait her turn to get a big part. We should award this to a senior," people complained. Somehow, I was still awarded the part. The drama coach taught me to speak with a low voice. I had short hair, was flat chested, and looked a bit like a boy. I danced, pranced, and did splits with ease, as I played this part. In rehearsals I made fast friends with many others. Mutti did not come to this performance, though, where I received many compliments. I guess she was too tired from her job.

Even though it was high school, not college, most of the incoming freshmen were invited to join sororities and fraternities. One group did offer me a spot, but I wasn't sure it was for me. So I asked Mutti, who cautioned me not to join. I was rejected from that group because I did not have the support of my parent. I befriended a small group of other "rejects" instead. There was Scott, who became an artist; Deidre, a vivacious dancer; and Karen and Hildy, my friends from dance camp. In the early 1950s, Scott was a rebel before anyone I knew. He wore his hair long and one afternoon, Principal Rice ordered him to have his hair cut. If he showed up the next day without a haircut, he'd be expelled. He showed up, with a dramatic mohawk haircut, two sides completely shaved and his long hair in the middle. We loved it. That Scott! He had done what Principal Rice asked, but in his own way. Another time, during lunch, a bully purposely spilled an entire bowl of tomato soup on Scott's shirt. Instead of being upset, he shouted, "Oh my goodness, I just got my first period!" This was the same Scott Burton whose sculptures can be seen all over Baltimore today.

At Western High, an art teacher named Leon Berkowitz took an interest in our little reject group. He invited us to his home on Kalorama Road where he lived with his wife, the poet Ida Fox. He talked to us about a lot of things, including politics, our goals in life, and the problems we faced at school. We had questions, and he would try to answer them. He was much influenced by the philosopher Martin Buber, and he shared his thoughts about Buber's writings. He asked us to draw things, and he analyzed the drawings. For example, he asked us to draw three trees, a road, and a fence. When I showed him my drawing, he told me that the middle tree symbolizes me, the tree on the left stood for my father, and the tree on the right was my mother. In my picture, my tree leaned heavily towards the left tree, in other words, towards my father. A fence was blocking the trees from the road, which made me think of the years in which I longed for my father. I was astounded at how accurate that interpretation was.

Mr. Berkowitz noticed that our little group was not accepted by the other students and he made sure we felt okay about who we were. He encouraged us in discussing books, poetry, philosophy, art, and dance. I remember spending most Saturdays at his little apartment home with my friends. He made us sandwiches. It felt good to spend time with a caring adult who believed in us, praised our strengths, advised us, and quoted from the Old Testament. He even met with Mutti and asked her how serious I was about dance. He thought I had art talent, which surprised both Mutti and me, and he suggested I might want to major in art in college. She assured him that my passion for dance was real. Later, Mr. Berkowitz made quite a name for himself as an artist in Washington, D.C.

The beginning of my sophomore year stood out because schools in Washington integrated for the first time. Many of these schools had problems with protests. At Western High School, later named Duke Ellington School of the Arts, there were only six Black students enrolled. There were no protests following their enrollment, but no one welcomed them either, except for our little group, which invited the newcomers to our homes. We took turns, each of us hosting one event. I knew what it felt like not to be welcomed. I knew how it felt to be judged by what one looks like instead of how one acted. I hope at least our little group made them feel welcome, as Deacon Harris and Mr. Berkowitz had done for us.

We also had physical education as a class, and part of this was a session on health. In it, we were lectured on the facts of life, which included encouragement to marry within one's own race. This was the key to a successful and happy marriage, we were told. I wondered whether I'd ever find a half- Chinese-half- German to marry, or was I destined to live alone? No one in our class asked any questions or seemed to be bothered by what the teacher was saying. It bothered me enough to go to the assistant principal, Mrs. Bowen, who used to be my French teacher whom I respected and liked. She laughed when I told her what we were taught. She assured me that it was nonsense and to ignore that advice.

In my junior year, my friends were excited about the things they were learning in Physics, so I asked if I could join them the following semester. When she found out I had not taken a single math class since junior high school, she refused, saying it would be incredibly difficult with no high school math experience. But that year, I had a good history teacher and for the first time, I was interested in the subject. But because I had tuned out all my other history classes, I was a disaster, never able to put historic events together chronologically. I wished I'd had a giant stack of classic comic books on history to fill me in. Those books summarized events in a short and concise manner, a lazy way to absorb facts painlessly.

At home, on some evenings, we would sit and read a play aloud. Mutti and I took female roles, while George and Henri took the male roles. Many nights we read Shakespeare, and I grew to love his plays. Mutti suggested I cook every Wednesday night, which included shopping for the groceries I needed and cooking the entire meal. It was a challenge, for which I prepared all week. Usually, the meal turned out well. Unfortunately, I had a hard time breaking this rhythm and after I married, my young husband and I discovered I needed an entire week to prepare a single meal.

CHAPTER SEVEN

Honor

I didn't do well in most team sports during my physical education class, but I ran fast and easily cleared the high jump, no matter how high the bar was placed. I looked forward to the end of school competition, held in May 1954. We had no track team but our coach would improvise a version of a high jump. He would place a bar across two poles, and everyone would have to jump over it. The height would keep increasing, and most of the students would knock it over, except for me and my biggest competition, Margie. This year, I was eager to determine exactly how high I could go. When competition day finally came, I invited my then boyfriend Roger Lee to come cheer me on. We had dated for a while. Roger was a sweet boy from a wealthy Shanghainese family. He was sent to the United States to study engineering. Many of my Chinese friends berated me with taunts like, "Why are you dating a rich boy? Yuck!" These taunts came from Confucian wisdom we all were taught from early childhood about how valued each profession was in the eyes of the Chinese:

1. If you want the greatest respect, become a scholar or educator.
2. If you don't have the smarts or the ambition to study, become a farmer.
3. If you don't have the smarts nor the desire for the hard work of farming, become a soldier.
4. The lowest on the list is a merchant, a money maker and businessman who is shown the least respect.

These values were standard for the Chinese for years, and guided Chinese people in place of an organized religion. Confucian values left out the lowest of the low, the almost unmentionables: performers, actors, musicians, dancers, and professional beggars.

Everyone at that time looked down on the rich. My friends thought they were looking out for me by encouraging me to avoid this son of a merchant. But Roger was not like that. He did not flaunt his wealth. He was kind, he was funny, and he was good company. He was ready and willing to help anyone with anything.

On competition day, Roger agreed to come support me. First was the one-hundred-yard dash. My competitor Margie was short, strong, and popular. She and I quickly moved way ahead of all the others and were neck and neck. The whole school shouted out, "Margie! Margie! Margie!" Maybe Roger was cheering for me, but his voice was drowned out by the others clamoring for Margie to win. In the end, I won by a hair. I was upset that everyone preferred Margie to win, so maybe I pushed harder.

Later came the high jump. Everyone else had knocked down the bar, and only Margie and I were left. I was excited. Just how high could I jump? On my last jump, I sprang up and came down hard on my wrist. I heard the crack and sharp pain pierced through me. I couldn't get up. An ambulance was called, and they took me to the nearby hospital to set my broken wrist. Margie, bless her heart, knocked down the bar on her turn, so that we both tied for first place. Having a cast on my arm was wonderful in that I did not have to wash dishes for six weeks. Unfortunately, it also meant that I couldn't play the violin with our orchestra at the senior class graduation. Mrs. Dwight Eisenhower, the First Lady, would be attending the ceremony because her nephew or grand-nephew was graduating. I was furious at myself for being so clumsy. I wanted to be the concertmistress in that performance, and now with a cast I wasn't able to play at all. But Mr. Nicodemus suggested I conduct the orchestra at this performance instead. I did, and in the middle of our opening piece, I turned around to face the audience so Mamie Eisenhower could see me. What a ham and show off I was. Still am.

Shortly after school was done, Joan came home to announce her plans to marry her sixty-year-old professor. She was barely twenty. Mutti was furious. When Joan was a young freshman at Bennington College, she was earning extra money babysitting for her dynamic, charismatic elderly professor of music, Paul Boepple. He had two small boys with his third wife. Paul became enamored with this young, talented student of his who, perhaps missing a father figure in her life, also fell for her mentor and teacher.

For Joan's sophomore year, Mutti made her transfer to the University of Michigan to get her away from this unsuitable relationship, but this didn't work. Joan and Paul continued to see each other despite the distance. Joan returned to Bennington the following year. Paul divorced his young wife; and upon Joan's graduation, they traveled together to be married at the courthouse in D.C. As angry as Mutti was, there was nothing she could do but welcome Paul into our family.

As for my summer, dance took up most of my time and energy. My teachers had scheduled a major performance for the seven top dancers at the studio, and we were to perform at some big event. I was given the best part. Three weeks before our major performance, Ms. Nirenska received a notice from the managers of the National Theater where Rodgers and Hammerstein's *The King and I* was playing. The show had completed many years on Broadway and now the Broadway company was performing in a road tour around the United States. One of the dancers had just dropped out, and they needed to find a replacement. An audition was being held in New York. However, the manager of the National Theater had seen some local D.C. dancers who he thought might be good enough, so he alerted all the studios to send their best dancers who were under five foot three for an audition the next Saturday. Ms. Nirenska took me aside and said, "Katherine, there is going to be an audition at the National Theater next Saturday. You don't qualify because you are much too tall, but I think the experience of an audition would be good for you." I agreed to go for the experience. I arrived at the theater along with about twenty other dancers. One of them was my classmate, Sally, who was with me at Leon Fokine's. She had been chosen to be in his company, while I had dropped out from his studio over a year before. We were happy to see each other. A man with a clipboard came around and asked each of us to give him our name, phone number, and height.

"My name is Katherine Hsu. My phone number is EM3-4579. I am five foot six."

"I'll write down that you are five foot three," he said. I didn't understand why he said that, but I said, "Okay." I had not paid attention to my teacher's comment about height.

That night I was babysitting. Around nine o'clock the phone rang; it was Mutti. She told me to phone a man from *The King and I* company. She sounded excited but didn't tell me why. I called him up to discover I had been chosen to be a member of *The King and I* company! The bosses at my first professional job were Richard Rodgers and Oscar Hammerstein! Really?! I was ecstatic! I would be paid one hundred and fifty dollars a week.

I was to begin rehearsal the following Monday, and had to be ready to perform the Wednesday after that. I couldn't wait to tell Ms. Nirenska. It didn't occur to me that by agreeing to be in this new company, I could no longer perform with Ms. Nirenska's group, and our upcoming performance in two weeks would have to be canceled, because I had the main part. There wasn't an understudy. The composition of the group couldn't be changed at this late date. All I could think about was that my dream of becoming a professional dancer had come true. I hadn't begun my senior year of high school, but I didn't care. School wasn't important. Dancing is what I'd always wanted to do.

The next day, I called Ms. Nirenska and excitedly told her the news. There was silence on the phone. A long silence.

She ordered me to come to the studio immediately. I couldn't understand it. Why wasn't she happy for me? She was the one who sent me to the audition.

Running downhill to the studio eight blocks from my home, I arrived breathless, on cloud nine. She opened her door and ushered me in. In a stern and cold voice, she lectured me for what felt like two hours. She spoke about honor. I was to honor my obligation to her. She had given me the biggest part in the upcoming dance performance. We had been working for weeks, the seven other dancers and I. By joining the new company and abandoning the old group, I would be letting her down, as well as my friends. She told me I was talented and there would be many, many other opportunities to dance. This time, I would have to turn *The King and I* down. She said I owed her. She had invested three years in my training, never charging my mother a penny. I was a good dancer because of her. It was my duty to stay and perform with her group and turn this job down. I walked out of the studio completely shaken.

I thought about all that she'd said and I understood her disappointment. I knew the other dancers would be upset with me. But there was no way I was going to turn this job down. It was an opportunity of a lifetime. I felt extremely guilty upsetting the person who spent the most time and energy with me, who believed in me and trained me. I became a strong dancer only because of her faith in me. I loved her and felt horrible about disappointing her. I took the part and she never spoke to me again, and I've continued to feel badly about it to this day.

CHAPTER EIGHT

The King and I

For the next three weeks, I lived at home and took public transportation for the rehearsals and performances for *The King and I*. The buses were unreliable, and I was late for one rehearsal and, unbelievably, I forgot another. The dance captain, Joan Fitzmaurice, was not pleased and cautioned me not to be late again, nor miss a rehearsal, or I would be docked. In hindsight, I've chalked my delinquency up to the fact that I was barely seventeen and my sense of responsibility had not yet set in.

I took my first paycheck, the amazing sum of one hundred and fifty dollars, to go shopping at the Lord and Taylor department store. When I had gone there before with my hard-earned babysitting money, consisting of ten dollars or so, I'd buy a fairly nice skirt for five dollars; but all around me were so many clothes I longed for but couldn't afford. This time, I walked up and down the aisles all afternoon because I could afford to buy whatever I wanted. It felt stupendous. But strangely, now that

I could buy it, nothing appealed to me. I couldn't find a single blouse or skirt that looked good enough to buy, and I went home without having spent a single penny.

The 126 *King and I* cast and crew members were welcoming and kind to me. They gave me all sorts of advice. Several cautioned me not to be quick to choose a roommate when the company went to other cities to perform, even though hotel rooms were much cheaper with a roommate to split the cost. They advised me to get to know the cast better so I'd choose someone with whom I would get along. Choosing hastily, and having to dissolve the living arrangement, becomes tricky and unpleasant. Somewhat like a mini divorce. They also taught me how to put on makeup, along with the sequence of my seven costume changes and how to do them quickly.

They told me Yul Brynner, who had played the king for years, finally left the show in order to play that part in the play's movie adaptation. Brynner, they said, was a great actor and gave acting workshops in the Stanislavski method to the cast. This method is made up of various techniques designed to allow actors to create believable characters. However, Brynner had a foul temper, my castmates explained. He supposedly had three different Annas fired, which cost the company a fortune. All the fired Annas had to be paid their salaries for the remainder of the run of the shows, which ran on Broadway for a handful of years. I was glad that I didn't have to deal with the temperamental artist.

They also taught me how to apply to the Actors' Equity Union. Life as a professional without a union was horrible, they said. One dancer who had been a member of a circus told me they traveled all night on a train, arrived at a new town, got out, set up tents, got dressed, performed, had supper, performed again, and then packed up after several nights and rode the train to the next town. It was a grueling job without union regulations and safeguards, which would've guaranteed them time to rest between shows, and made sure working hours were not excessive.

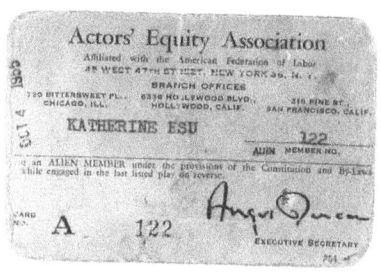

Some performers had been members of the Radio City Music Hall Rockettes. There they barely had time to run out for lunch with makeup still on, then rush back to perform again without time to rest.

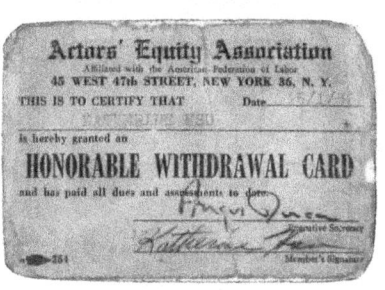

Katherine's Actors' Equity cards

They hated that job. But with Actors' Equity, the rehearsal hours were set. The dancers would have to be given time off after a certain number of hours of work. Life, my fellow performers told me, was ever so much better with a union looking out for them.

In our last week in D.C., one dancer dropped out and a dancer from New York joined us. Her name was Aileen Passloff and she didn't ask anyone for advice because she had been in other shows and already knew the routines. Because she didn't ask anyone for help, everyone decided Aileen was stuck up and ignored her. However, I liked her immediately. On the third day, I ignored the advice I was given and asked her if she'd be my roommate when the company traveled to Baltimore. She agreed. The other dancers were worried I had made a terrible mistake, but I hadn't. It was one of the best decisions I'd ever made.

Aileen had graduated from Bennington College, whereas most company members did not even attend college. At one point, Aileen explained homosexuality to me because many of the male dancers were gay. I had no idea. I was raised very naive.

The previous year I had a pair of parakeets that I had hoped would reproduce, so I asked a neighbor boy who raised parakeets how they mated and had eggs. Do they rub beaks? Was that how baby parakeets were made? I guess he thought I was joking because he didn't answer. The only other pets I raised were crickets who sang and lived in a little wooden cage in Chongqing. And cicadas that my sister and I caught by making a net using a soft twig made into a circle attached to a broom handle. We then dipped the rounded twig onto many spider webs so we had a really sticky surface. We would then place this sticky web onto the back of each cicada sitting on a tree trunk, remove the lovely singing bug, and place him in a jar. Later, we would empty this jar into the mosquito curtain hanging from the ceiling above my bed. I would have forty cicadas singing to me while I slept! But none of these pets helped me to understand how they reproduced. Then I asked Mutti how babies were made. All she told me was, "Look at your silkworms."

I had been raising silkworms at home, feeding them mulberry leaves and watching them grow from these tiny little fuzzy black worms that were barely visible, to white shiny two-to three-inch beautiful worms that took three days weaving these lovely cocoons for themselves; after a couple of weeks inside the cocoon, they would emerge as moths.

These moths would have short wings with which to flap until they found a mate. Then, using the ends of their bodies, the moths would hook end-to-end with a fellow moth, holding on to it for hours. Conception having occurred, after disengaging the females would go on to lay many eggs, which I would save until the next spring to hatch and start the whole process of feeding the babies mulberry leaves again.

So when Mutti explained how babies were made by telling me to look at my silkworms, it didn't make much sense. End to end? Did Baba and Mutti put their behinds together for a long time to make babies? That seemed weird to me. In the end, it was Aileen who answered these questions. When I asked her if she had ever made love, she wouldn't tell.

One afternoon at rehearsal, we had to practice rolling while the dancer who played Simon Legree "kicked" us. It was not a real kick, but was meant to look like one to the audience. We needed to perfect that sequence in Uncle Tom's Cabin, a dance within the show. We crouched on the floor, arms around our bent knees, and rolled over and over. For about twenty minutes we rolled and rolled. My back began to ache excruciatingly. The next day I went to an orthopedic doctor who took x-rays. He told me I had spondylolisthesis. This is a condition in which there is slippage between vertebrae in the lower spine. It's possible to live a lifetime without problems, but by rolling and rolling, I had displaced a vertebra into the gap, which caused severe pain. He told me I should never do that movement again. Further, he suggested I drop out of the company and never dance again. I returned to the hotel, devastated, sobbing. Aileen listened to my report and decided that we should ask our dance captain if I could beg out of that particular segment of the performance. The dance captain was understanding and relieved me from that dance. Thanks to Aileen, I continued to see doctors in each of the cities the show traveled to, in order to ensure my back would be okay.

The next week, as I walked around town I met a couple of Chinese sailors. They spoke to me, and when I found out they were from Taiwan and would be returning there soon, I asked if I could send a gift to my father, his new wife Nancy, and their baby boy, Alex, who had just been born. The sailors agreed and invited me to bring my gift to their ship the next afternoon. That evening I told my fellow dancers about meeting the sailors. My friends suggested I buy a push-up bra so I would look sexier to make the sailors happy. I had never heard of a push-up bra. The next morning, I went to a department store and tried one on. It was amazing. Even with my tiny breasts, wearing that bra I saw

Katherine with Taiwanese sailors who delivered a gift on Katherine's behalf to her father, his new wife, and their baby

cleavage, so I bought it, along with a toy kangaroo with a baby joey in her pouch for my new half-brother, Alex. When I got to the ship, all the sailors wanted a photo with me, so I posed for many photos. I gave my dad's address to the sailors I befriended and am pleased to say they delivered the kangaroo to my dad's new baby on their return to Taiwan.

When I arrived at the theater that night for the performance, the dance captain stopped me in my tracks. "You forgot to come to rehearsal again today, Katherine." I was so thrilled about the sailors and the ship that I'd totally neglected to keep track of the rehearsal time. "I'm so sorry, it won't happen again, I promise."

"Don't bother getting makeup, you are to go home. Your salary will be docked for today." I'd finally done it–I'd really messed up. Even worse was what I learned later from my former ballet classmate Sally, from Leon Fokine's studio, who had joined our company a week earlier. Mr. and Mrs. Fokine had driven from Washington to see their two dancers perform. Sally explained that when she told Mr. Fokine after the performance that I had missed a rehearsal and was sent home, he said, "I knew it, I always knew she was unreliable. I'm glad I kicked her out of our company."

That event was devastating, yet mentally galvanizing, and I have never, ever been late for anything since. All the nightmares I've had since then are ones in which I was lost and late. The guilt plagues me still. That day I returned to my hotel full of shame, took out my violin and played my heart out. I played the pieces I loved the best. Hearing the sounds emanating from my violin was comforting. It made me feel a bit better.

When we performed in Baltimore, a strange thing happened. Almost every night as I exited backstage, among the signature seekers was a group of Chinese who were waiting for me with invitations for dinner. It turned out that the Chinese community felt my mother had made a terrible mistake allowing me to perform on stage with, according to Confucian ideology, the "degenerate folks," the sing song dancers. The Chinese community felt it would do me harm to associate with the cast members. At just seventeen years old, I didn't know much about professional actors, singers, or dancers. I didn't know how they might influence me. These were adults whom I had to respect. Therefore, almost every day some Chinese family would have me over for early supper. The larger Chinese community sought to keep me safe and away from bad influences, and many of them wrote to their friends and relatives in the towns where the show was headed. As a result, I could count on receiving invitations for meals in most cities, many times hosted by Chinese friends of friends. My *King and I* friends asked me how I dared to accept strangers' invitations into their homes. I told them I trusted them because they were Chinese. My instincts were absolutely right. All of them treated me with kindness and generosity.

After two weeks of performances in Baltimore, the company traveled to Pittsburgh. My boyfriend Roger drove up and bought tickets for every show. One day he sent a beautiful corsage of a fragrant white gardenia that was delivered to my dressing table at the theater. It was lovely, and I wore it as I exited backstage. Roger, as usual, was there to escort me back to the hotel. One of my dancer friends said to Roger, "Hey, that was a really sweet gift for Katherine. How about sending a corsage to the rest of us?" Quite the surprise greeted us at the next performance! There, on every single dressing table, was a gardenia corsage; there was one for every member of the show. Everyone, all 126 members of the cast and crew, exited backstage wearing the corsage, and laughed, saying they looked like members of a convention. It never occurred to me how much Roger must have spent to impress my friends and me. I was just flattered to have his devotion.

Roger had also given me some gifts prior to this. Mutti had cautioned me not to accept such gifts because it meant I was serious about our relationship. I ignored Mutti, as usual. I liked presents and I knew I wasn't serious. He was just one of the boys I went out with. Chinese boys were always very respectful. Holding hands was as far as we went; kissing was reserved for engaged couples.

While we were in Pittsburgh, the stage managers held auditions for understudies. They were looking for an understudy for Simon Legree, the evil one in Uncle Tom's Cabin, and one for the main singer-actress, Anna.

I decided to audition for both, remembering Mrs. Nirenska's theory that auditioning is always a good experience. When auditioning for Simon Legree, I had to wear his mask. It was large and heavy. I knew the dance for the part but wearing the mask felt awkward. I didn't think I did that well. But that afternoon the dance captain Joan Fitzmaurice took me aside and said, "Katherine, Jerome Robbins, our choreographer, was at the show last night looking for dancers for the movie they are filming in Hollywood. He told me that last month two dancers from Thailand had auditioned. They were terrific but he couldn't hire them because they'd make every other dancer look bad! He also said the only dancer he saw last night that he wanted for the movie was you. I told him you were five foot six, which disappointed him because it was necessary to be under five foot three in order for all the dancers to look the same height."

She continued, "As for today's tryout for Simon Legree, you should get the understudy part because you were the best dancer. This job would mean a salary increase, but you are brand new to the company, and I think I should give the part to the next best dancer. She has been with the show for over three years." I agreed, and thanked Ms. Fitzmaurice, surprised and flattered by what she had said.

When I tried out for the role of Anna's understudy, my friends laughed. "If you earned the part, Katherine, they would have to change the story from an English woman traveling to Siam (now Thailand) to teach the King's children, to a Siamese teacher traveling to England to teach the British king's kids!" We both laughed at that idea. In this audition I was asked to sing one of Anna's songs, so I sang "Shall I Tell You What I Think of You?"

After I sang, one of the managers sitting in the audience of the theater said, "Katherine, you have a nice voice. You should take singing lessons; they will help you to project your voice." Several of my friends in the wing told me I had done a clever thing. I showed off my versatility to the managers who would probably be managing other shows later on. I could not only dance, I could also sing. That had not been my plan. I simply auditioned for the experience, and it was fun.

Hartford, Connecticut was the next town on our tour. Henri had an elderly woman friend who lived there, in Mark Twain's old home, and gave tours of it during the day. I spent an afternoon learning about Twain and his family with this friend of Henri's. I remember seeing the porch of this grand home made to look like a ship's deck, replete with a replica of a ship's steering wheel. In Mark Twain's bedroom there were beautiful dresses that had belonged to his wife, and dolls that his children had played with. I had loved his books, and this visit to his home made me love him even more.

In the Hartford hotel, Aileen and I were given a room on the third floor with large windows facing the street. We felt quite private and at ease in that room, but one morning as I was coming out of the shower, walking to the dresser where my clothes were, I happened to look out of the window and saw several men across the street in a dry-cleaning factory, looking through binoculars that were zeroed in on our window. I quickly ducked down low and screamed, "Peeping Toms are watching us!" Aileen, who was also getting dressed, crouched down, then scooted and crawled over to the cords at the side of the windows to close the curtains. As if all of this wasn't bad enough, when we returned to our room that night at about 11 p.m., we found a "gift" outside our door from the dry-cleaning store. The gift package contained a couple of free hangers and a coupon for a cleaning discount. We panicked, thinking those creeps had figured out which room we were staying in. Later, we learned that all the hotel guests had received the same gift that night. By the time we had arrived back at the hotel, all the other guests must have already brought the gifts into their rooms, or tossed them in the trash, which was why our gift was the only one still sitting outside our room.

After a week in Hartford, we left for Boston on two trains. We went through a terrible storm on the way there, and we heard that one train with half our cast would be delayed. Those of us on the first train made it to Boston without incident. But there was no news on the others. We were all worried. Aileen was visiting a friend in Boston and I was alone in the hotel that night when I received a call from Joe, a singer who was on the delayed train.

"Are you okay? We were so scared for you and the other half of our cast."

It was late, around 1 a.m., but I was anxious to hear what happened, so I went to his room. He sat on his bed and invited me to sit with him. I did, and waited for him to tell me what he knew about our missing friends. His hand then reached up to my chest.

"What are you doing, Joe? You're married!" I jumped up and ran out of his room. I felt amazingly stupid. I should have known what he was up to, but I think being so incredibly naive somehow saved me.

The other performers ultimately made it to Boston without harm, and once we were all there, the managers rehearsed us for hours. They were concerned because the critics in Boston were exceptionally difficult to please, and they even hired professional photographers to take our photos during the rehearsal. In no other cities were we pressured to perform so perfectly. There was so much tension on opening night that in the middle of a dance, I completely blanked out. I stood still, panicking for three horrible seconds, as I could not remember what I was supposed to do next. Fortunately, I just stopped thinking. With my head empty and my heart racing, I just moved. It was peculiar. My body remembered what to do and made all the correct moves, even in the absence of all conscious thought. This still lingers as one of the weirdest moments in my life. I had been told about muscle memory, but this proved it to me.

Another time in Boston, I stopped at an outdoor newsstand where there were several racks of candy. I fingered one candy bar, set it down, and started to pick up another one, when the newsstand clerk yelled, "Hey kid, don't touch the candy unless you plan to buy it." The harsh shout startled me. Was it because I looked Asian? When the shame began creeping in my brain, I stopped and reminded myself not to allow others to make me feel badly about what I looked like or represented. It was a new beginning sparked by my growing confidence. I was soon to be eighteen, earning almost as much money as my mother.

The last place we traveled to was Philadelphia. The show was to play there for six weeks. Because of the long stay, Aileen and I found a nice apartment to rent. We had to put down a three-hundred-dollar security payment in case we damaged the apartment. Philadelphia is known as the city of brotherly love, and that is what we encountered. Aileen and I agreed that it was the nicest city we had been in. The museums were magnificent. Jack Carr, a classmate of Harris Collingwood, took me to many places in Philadelphia during our stay. He also introduced me to a sweet Chinese boy named Jack Chen, who also escorted me around and introduced me to his friends. During these six weeks, I turned eighteen. What surprised me was that being away from home, I didn't expect any sort of celebration for my birthday. But on my birthday, when I arrived at the theater, I found a pile of gifts from friends in the show on my dressing table. In the middle of that evening's show, Patricia Morrison, who played the lead, Anna, whispered, "happy birthday, Katherine." She said it right on stage as I danced near her. I was so touched!

The show was slated to end in Philadelphia. So, many dancers were looking into other job possibilities. I'd heard they were looking for a replacement for the lead in another show called *Teahouse of the August Moon*. When I went to audition for that part, the manager offered me the lead role if I went to bed with him. I couldn't believe my ears.

"You've got to be kidding. I'd never ever do that!" I answered.

"Just wait until you are hungry," he said as I walked out.

I discussed my options with Aileen. I could go to New York and audition for parts. Many people in the show urged me to do that, telling me I had the most talent of anyone in the show. But my dear friend Aileen urged me to go back home, finish high school, and attend college.

"Katherine, you should try college," she said, putting her hand on my shoulder. If you don't like it, you can always leave and go back to New York. On the other hand, if you go to New York now, you probably will never finish school and wonder for the rest of your life whether you should have gotten a college education." She convinced me and I decided to follow her advice. Aileen was the only one who advised me to get an education. She didn't think I was too stupid to succeed in school. In the mid 2000s, I went to see her in her studio apartment, and thanked her from the bottom of my heart for the advice, which positively changed the direction of my life.

At the last performance, the show's five singers put a sign on their bottoms under their huge skirts. As they finished the last number, they turned their backs to the audience, lifted their skirts, and on each behind was one word. Read from left to right, the sentence spelled, THIS IS THE END BABY! I smile now thinking of them doing this, knowing that they wouldn't get in trouble because the show's tour was over. We signed programs for each other—wishing each other good luck, praising one another's talent. As we prepared to leave the theater for the last time, each cast member took a memento or two from the costumes. It was expected and it was okay, so I took a necklace and an ankle band. My profession as a performing dancer finished that day, but I continued dancing and teaching dance for many more years.

Aileen left for New York the next day, as Jack and I finished cleaning the apartment. He offered to drive me home to Washington, D.C. Once we were done, we went to the landlord to get our security deposit back. The manager hesitated. He said he would mail the refund in a couple of weeks, which raised Jack's suspicions.

"You don't need to mail it, I will come to get it," Jack said in a firm voice. The manager looked at Jack, realized that he meant business, and immediately wrote me a check for the three hundred dollars. I will always be grateful to Jack for his astuteness and for his behavior. Later I had heard that Jack was quite a playboy, but he never tried anything funny with me. He was a perfect gentleman the whole time.

CHAPTER NINE

High School, Again

I accepted Jack's offer to drive me back to Washington, and once there, everything seemed different. It was now mid-December 1955; Mutti had gotten tired of taking care of my pet parakeets during my five months away and released them. George was so upset with her that she advertised in the local newspaper about lost parakeets. She planned to accept any parakeet that someone found and pretend they were mine, hoping I wouldn't notice. No one responded to her ad, but I didn't get angry about my lost parakeets. I had also matured during the months on my own. I knew taking care of the birds was a burden for Mutti. It pleased me to learn that George worried about Mutti's decision to release my parakeets out the window.

The next week after my return, I went to my high school and asked if there was any way I could still graduate with my class in June. They told me that before I could be accepted back to school, I had to study the civics manual on my own and take a test about the U.S. Constitution. If I passed, I'd get credit for that course and satisfy the requirement to enter as a senior class student. When the second semester began in late January, I would have to take all the required classes in order to graduate. These were two English classes, a French class, P.E., as well as my favorites—art, chorus, and orchestra. I was thrilled that even though I'd missed half of the year, I could still finish on time.

That Christmas, Mutti, as usual, bought a live tree and as was the German tradition, decorated it with real candles. She and Henri had married while I was touring and were quite happy together. That Christmas Eve, with gifts under the tree, we all dressed in our finest clothes. I had a pretty nylon dress with a full skirt, extended by a crinoline underneath. I felt very pretty as we began to light the candles on the tree. I bent down and lit the candles on the lowest branches since those were the closest to me. Then I lit the candles on the next tier up. As I continued lighting candles I had to reach high and into the tree to get the top candles. I didn't realize that the bottom of my pretty nylon dress was directly over the lowest candles. All of a sudden, I looked down and saw that the entire lower part of my dress was on fire. Too frightened to move, I stood rooted in place. No one had ever taught me to stop, drop, and roll; I just panicked and stood frozen. Henri had been lighting candles on the other side of the tree, saw my dress in flames, rushed over and, with his arms, began trying to put out the flames. Whap, whap, whap, whap...until the flames were gone. The bottom of my dress was also gone, but I was not burned. It never occurred to me to ask Henri whether he had any burns on his arms. I must have been in shock, because I just walked like a zombie to my bedroom, to change into another dress. My mother didn't seem the least concerned or upset that I was almost burned. Did she not care? Was it because Henri ended it before anyone was able to react? After that, at every Christmas, Henri begged Mutti not to use real candles on the tree, but she ignored him. Her German heritage was too important to her.

Back in town, having performed professionally and living on my own, my image changed among my friends. I was invited everywhere. Meanwhile, I had to study the civics textbook in order to be able to pass the final test and graduate with my class in June. But in the evenings, I was invited out on many dates. At parties, I challenged myself to see how many boys asked for my phone number. Flowers regularly arrived at our home from various suitors. Henri often worried that perhaps Mutti had a secret boyfriend. Henri had never been married before and he cherished Mutti. She thought it was so silly for him to imagine that the flowers were for her, and occasionally she'd tease him and make up an imaginary admirer.

At the Chinese parties, June Chung and I competed to see who was more popular. She was the sister of Connie Chung, the famous TV reporter.

In my diary, I wrote about several weekends where I had seven dates. Seven! I have since misplaced my old diary, but can remember the pattern going something like this: Friday night dinner and movies was one date. Then on Saturday, an after breakfast stroll through the nearby cemetery reading tombstones (quite interesting) was the second. Lunch with another date was third. Dinner and concert with another was fourth. A Sunday morning trip to the zoo would have been the fifth. Lunch with another boy, sixth. Sometimes I'd come home from the sixth date to find my seventh date waiting at the doorstep for dinner and the movies. That same scenario happened several times.

As I think back, when Mutti was tired and frustrated, she'd yell at me saying, "You're so awful, why would anyone like you?" I took it as fact. So the more dates I had, the more wedding proposals I received, and these proposals were validations for me that I wasn't awful, that someone liked me enough to take me out or even marry me. At that time, besides Lieutenant Li who had proposed when I was fifteen, three other boys, Hans, Roger and Francois, a French boy, had each proposed marriage to me. Was it because I swore to remain chaste until marriage?

When the second semester of high school began, I took the Civics test and passed. This time around in school, I focused on my classes and the rest of my schoolwork, because I did not want to go back to the dance studio where I had so upset the teachers. I was surprised by my classmates as they treated me as a minor celebrity, which felt great. Now the cheerleaders, the cool kids who had previously been quite nasty to me, stopped making snide remarks about my unpolished shoes or unfashionable clothes. I was featured in the school newspaper. I took an aptitude test to see what profession was most suitable for me. Although I don't remember all of the results, I do remember that the chart had one item that was so low it barely made a mark: secretarial work.

The school counselor met with me to discuss colleges. "Most colleges," she told me, "segregate freshmen girls. They have study hours every evening from seven to nine and curfew at ten. Because you have traveled and been on your own, I believe you would find these rules too restrictive, so there are two colleges that I think might suit you better and that you might like. One is Bucknell University in Pennsylvania. And the other is

St. John's in Annapolis, Maryland." I remembered that Harris Collingwood, my deacon, had loved St. John's and graduated from there before attending seminary to become a priest. All along Mutti had indicated that she thought I was not bright enough for college. Also, colleges were expensive. Mutti could not afford it. However, I had saved a good deal from my earnings at *The King and I*. My church pastor had also mentioned that the church could help me financially if I decided to attend college. I thought about my roommate Aileen's encouragement to try college for a year and see.

I took the school counselor's advice and made plans to visit both Bucknell and St. John's. After a short stay at Bucknell, I left on the bus to St. John's College, nicknamed the "Great Books College," where I stayed for two days. Unlike all the talk about boys and the upcoming exams at Bucknell University, the girls at St. John's mostly talked about their classes and what they were learning. There were 161 students in the whole college, both boys and girls, all of whom had to take the same classes during their four years. At that time, there was only one Black student and one Asian student. The professors, who were called "tutors," in the British style, had to teach every class offered at the college, in addition to their main class. That means if the professor had his PhD in mathematics, he taught math, but also needed to study Ancient Greek or chemistry, or music, later German, French, or biology. On and on until he was able to teach any of the classes taught in all four years! In this way, if students in biology class mentioned something they learned in music class, the tutor would know that because he had also taught music. If a student in French class mentioned something she learned in Ancient Greek class, or about Euclidean geometry, that tutor would understand the student's references. I thought this was impressive. I visited the small classes of fourteen to seventeen students. There were no lectures, only discussions, where the students took equal parts with the tutor. It was wonderful, and I wanted to attend.

In 1955, attending college was a privilege for most high schoolers in the United States. Although the cost was not prohibitive, a college degree was not a necessity for obtaining a well paying job. It was looked upon by many as a luxury not worth attaining.

I then met with the St. John's College admissions director, James Tolbert. He immediately took a liking to me. Maybe it was because his eldest daughter, Linda, aspired to be a professional dancer. He accepted me immediately for the fall. Bless him, he didn't need me to take the SAT and didn't need to see any of my report cards. He told me that with a college degree, one had a much greater chance of a good paying job. The college would give me a generous scholarship and a student aid job to work in his office, as well as serve as hostess to any visiting prospective student. The college encouraged prospective students to spend a few days on campus attending classes. That was a smart approach because the classes were truly exciting, unlike most colleges, which simply offered lectures and exams. I was ecstatic. I made friends during that initial visit with one boy in particular, John Chase. He took me out to see *Antigone*, a play performed at Bryn Mawr College in Pennsylvania. He had borrowed a car from a tutor, Winfree Smith, and we drove several hours to see the terrific play. The plan was for John to come get me in D.C. and to drive us to Pennsylvania to see the play, drive me back home, and then for John to return to Annapolis.

On the way back, John forgot to turn on his lights, and a car rear-ended us on the highway. At the moment of impact, the front seats dropped several inches. In 1956, no one had seat belts, but fortunately we were okay. John exchanged insurance information with the other driver and somehow he managed to drive us back to Annapolis to Winfree Smith's home, where John had to tell him that his car was damaged in an accident. Winfree was not only a tutor at the college but also a priest at St. Anne's Episcopal Church in Annapolis. That night, Reverend Smith allowed me to stay on his living room couch, as it was too late to get me back home to D.C. John went back to his dorm. The next day I took the bus home. I was leery of riding in cars for months after that. Every loud sound startled and frightened me.

In May, I invited John to be my date to my high school prom. He was so elegant. John had played the part of Ferdinand in *The Tempest* at St. John's earlier that year, which was a perfect part for this handsome boy.

Before college, I had a job the first six weeks of summer as a counselor at a girls' camp in Vermont called Camp Wyoda. It was my first experience in a camp setting and my role was to teach dance every morning for two hours. The rest of the day I was free, and I took advantage of my free hours to attend as many classes with the campers as I could. It was a joy to learn to ride a horse and to make baskets, jewelry, and other crafts.

One evening, a large group of the counselors decided to sneak out to a swimming hole.

"What? Leave our cabins? Leave our camper kids all alone?" The others convinced me that the kids would all be asleep. We'd leave at 11 p.m., well after their bedtime, and they'd be fine.

*Katherine and campers at Camp Wyoda in Vermont,
where Katherine worked as a counselor*

So at the appointed time, I quietly got out of bed, dressed, and met the others down by the flagpole. About a dozen of us crammed into a car and drove to a nearby lake. The others went skinny-dipping. Not me. I was too shy. They shared some bottles of beer. I didn't do that, either. It felt both fun and scary because I knew we should not have left our little campers without any supervision. What if one had a nightmare? Or became homesick?

After an hour or two of fun, we drove back to the camp and each of us crept back into our bunk, hoping no one noticed our disappearance. About thirty minutes later, I heard someone coming into my cabin.

"Is everything okay?" I said to whoever was standing there in the dark. I sat up, thinking it was one of my friends who had sneaked out with me.

It wasn't one of my friends, it was the woman who owned the camp! She put her head within two inches of my mouth, smelling my breath. "Where have you been?"

"I've been right here in bed with my campers, ma'am," hoping she couldn't detect the fear in my lie. She left without saying a word. Good thing I didn't taste any beer that night.

At the end of the summer, the church sent me on a week's retreat to a place in Virginia called Shrine Mont, in the Shenandoah Valley near the George Washington National Forest, to strengthen our faith. It was so enchanting that I vowed one day to have my wedding in the beautiful outdoor chapel there.

Ironically, when I planned my wedding two years later, I learned that because I was half-Asian, I was considered colored, and it was against the law for me to marry a white boy in Virginia. It never dawned on me that as an Asian, according to Virginia law, I was not good enough to marry a white man. That law was finally overturned in the mid 1960s. To think that in the U.S. for so long interracial marriages were a thing to avoid at all costs. What were the lawmakers afraid of? Why couldn't people marry who they loved? Why would anyone care about the color of one's skin or the slant of one's eyes? At that time I hadn't known that for decades the U.S. had laws that prohibited any Chinese to enter the country. What was it exactly that people here disliked or feared?

One of the first activities at the retreat was an icebreaker, a get-to-know each other game. All the students gathered in a large recreation room and the leaders, who were Episcopal clergymen, had names of well-known people, places, or things written on cards. They attached a card to the back of each student, and our job was to walk around and ask different kids yes or no questions about the cards on our backs.

Before the game began, I noticed one priest at the far end of the room who kept staring at me. Once the rules of the game were explained, the priests got up from their seats and began to place cards on our backs. This particular priest who had his eyes on me, ran across the room to tack his card on my back before another leader did. I wondered why it was so important to have that particular card. And I had to ask many questions before I finally found out. The card said, "Snake who tempted Adam and Eve."

Even now I wonder what the priest had in mind when he put that card on my back. Did he see me as a temptress? Did he see me as Evil? Was it because I was Chinese? It happened so long ago, but it still bothers me to this day.

CHAPTER TEN

Starting College

September could not come fast enough. I took the bus to Annapolis with my old *King and I* suitcase, which unfortunately reeked of dried urine from our cat Neko, who joined our family when Mutti married Henri. I was assigned a single room in Campbell Hall, a girls' dormitory. The room had two beds; one was for me, and one was for any prospective female student who might arrive to spend a few days at the college. My student aid job was to escort this student to breakfast and each of her assigned classes, and to introduce her to the tutors. After each class I was to find her and take her to her next class. At lunch, I was to sit with her and introduce her to others at the round tables in the dining hall, where all the students ate. I was to make her feel comfortable and welcomed.

Up until then, I had been fairly shy when dealing with strangers. But this job forced me to overcome that. When I had no prospective students to tend to, I was to spend a few hours with

Mr. Tolbert in his admissions office, either stuffing envelopes or in the Addressograph office typing name plates. Sometimes I filed papers, but that was really hard for me as I never learned to be comfortable with the alphabet, having learned it so late in my schooling. For each item, I had to recite the alphabet from A to Z until I came to the letter to see if it goes before or after the letters in the file drawer. No wonder my aptitude test showed I wouldn't be successful at secretarial jobs.

Sometimes I was asked to put mail in bags for the post office. If there were not enough letters to fill a bag for a single state, I was to put mail for neighboring states together. The problem with this was that I had no idea of the geography of the United States. It wasn't just the U.S., as I wasn't good with the geography of China either. When there was a batch of letters for Florida, I placed them in the same bag as letters for California because I knew oranges came from both states. By my logic, this made sense. I blush now just thinking about how stupid the Post Office must have thought St. Johnnies were when they opened that bag.

When I stuffed envelopes, I had a pile of them on one side of the desk and several piles of books in between. On the other side of the desk were the pile of letters to go in the envelopes. It simply didn't occur to me to move things in order to be more efficient, so it took me forever to fill them until Mr. Tolbert came by and moved all the books between the papers and the envelopes; with that done, the job went much faster and smoother.

When I had a guest, though, I'd wake up in the morning, jump out of bed, open the curtains and shout, "What a beautiful morning this is!" I loved getting up in the morning, and always woke up happy. As soon as my sleepy roommate heard my comment, she'd inevitably respond with, "UUUGGGGGGGGGH!" I found this strange until the reverse happened. One morning, my new roommate got up before I did, threw open the curtains and shouted,

"My God, it is beautiful outside!"

I found myself uttering, "UUUUGGGGGGGGH!" I had never uttered this. Is it possible for two happy people in the same room to jump up and greet the morning at the same time? I guess not.

I loved my student aid job and I loved all my classes. The seminar reading of Plato, Plotinus, and Aristotle's work was interesting, but no matter how many times I read the assignment, I never felt that I'd read it enough. Other seminars were fascinating. I loved my Ancient Greek and music classes. The biology teacher didn't like me, and didn't like my questions. Euclidean geometry made absolutely no sense because I hadn't had math classes since the eighth grade. A couple of classmates had to help me practically every single evening.

The third week of college I saw a notice for auditions for *King Lear*, my favorite of Shakespeare's plays. I went to the student director, Ray Haas, and asked him not to call on me the first day because I don't read aloud well until I've practiced. The tryouts were held over two days, and could he please allow me to read on the second day? I looked at Mr. Haas with his dark eyes, so intense, so piercing. I heard that he planned to play the part of Lear. I thought that I should try out for Cordelia, because in the final scene, Ray would have to carry me, crying. He was so attractive that I thought being carried by him would be cool. Mr. Haas, however, disregarded my request. I had to read that first day and I was not happy. Without practice, I didn't do well.

I don't know if I would have gotten a part even if I had read on the second day. It was all moot, though, because three days after auditions the play was canceled. I never did learn why.

Freshman biology class at the college was taught by an elderly man, Wiley Crawford, who had been there for many years. I felt an immediate antipathy from him. He did not understand how overjoyed I was at being in college, how I planned to do my very best in every single class to prove to my mother that I could succeed, and that I was not too stupid to be where I was.

One of the first biology experiments was to demonstrate that there are many semipermeable membranes in our bodies through which certain things pass. Mr. Crawford showed us a balloon made of this type of membrane (without explaining its properties) and filled it with a sugar solution, then placed it in a tank filled with water. We waited until the next class a few days later, and then we tested the water to find it contained sugar.

"How did that happen?" Mr. Crawford asked.

I enthusiastically jumped in, "Maybe there is a leak in that balloon."

Mr. Crawford was furious. He thought I was making a joke. He shouted something at me that greatly diminished my eagerness to contribute my ideas or questions. Up until that moment, I had understood the whole philosophy at the college was for all classes to be conducted as discussions where exchanges between tutors and students were encouraged and welcomed. But after that interaction with Mr. Crawford, I kept quiet for weeks. Then one day when he was naming the fins of fish, I was confused between the dorsal, caudal, and pectoral. I asked, "Which fin is the one that faces heaven?"

Maybe I should have said, "upwards" because he shouted at me again.

The entire rest of the course I kept quiet to keep myself safe from his wrath. I wondered if it were my questions he loathed or my ethnicity.

I befriended a scholarship student from China who needed student aid. He was assigned to work with the grounds crew who were all Black. There were no Black tutors on the faculty. Movie theaters, restaurants, and water fountains were all segregated. There was only one Black student. All his classmates liked him and wanted to have him join them in the bars, coffee shops, and restaurants, but he was never allowed in. In downtown Annapolis, there was a public bathroom in the square at the dock. There were separate entrances marked FOR WHITES ONLY and FOR COLORED ONLY. I wondered if I should just pee in between the two doors. College was about broadening one's horizons, but all around me race remained a limiting factor.

There was one exception to the discussion format at St. John's. Friday night lectures were the only lecture of the week. They were presented for the entire faculty and students. They were special, in part because everyone dressed up for the hour-long lectures, and also because of the interesting question and answer sessions that were held afterwards. In my dorm, there was a striking girl from India. She was one of the few non-white students at the college. She occasionally wore a sari to these lectures. Another girl and I told her how we admired the multicolor, shimmery, silk fabric, and she offered to lend each of us a sari to wear for the lecture one Friday.

Friday night came and she taught us to tuck one end of this long fabric into our half-slip to hold it there. Then she began to wrap the cloth around our bodies covering us entirely until the fabric was draped over one shoulder. We looked in the mirror and liked what we saw. The three of us walked towards the Great Hall where the lectures were held, but halfway there, I stepped on the bottom of my sari and the entire cloth fell off my body. There I stood, in my bra and half-slip, with the shimmery sari on the ground. There were students all around, on their way to the lecture, and I stood there mortified. But my two friends picked up the sari and quickly wrapped me up, and we dashed back in the dorm to put the sari on properly again. This time I walked more carefully, making sure I did not step on the bottom of the cloth. I blush now as I remember this scene.

At the end of the third month, freshmen students were each assigned to write a long paper. I had never learned to write papers well, and so when I was done, I went to Bob Bart, a tutor that Harris Collingwood liked, for help. Mr. Bart, who was also my seminar leader, spent hours upon hours with me, explaining and correcting my grammar. When we were finally done, he handed me my paper and said, "Well, Katherine, you now have a horrible paper that is perfectly grammatical." We spent so much time fixing the grammar that we had no more time, nor energy, to fix the content. I then knew that writing would be a constant struggle for me. Perhaps it was because English was my sixth language, after Mandarin, the Chongqing and Shanghainese dialects of Chinese, Italian, and French.

During my second semester, I developed more confidence. I didn't feel I had to rush back to my dorm after every class to study and do homework, so I signed up for some extracurricular activities such as chorus, directed by Victor Zuckerkandl. He noticed I had a strong alto voice, but didn't realize I had a limited range. For the spring concert, Mr. Zuckerkandl gave me a solo part within a melodious piece by Palestrina. I was honored to sing that part but it ended with a couple of high notes that I could not reach with a clear, strong voice; instead it came out as weak and screechy. In rehearsals, I began my solo well, but I always ended it poorly. Then at the concert, just two seconds before I began my solo, another girl sang my part. I was both surprised and relieved. Several friends came to me later and took my side saying, "How dare she steal your solo?!" I was glad Mr. Zuckerkandl asked her to take over, but it felt good to have friends to support me and who thought I had been slighted.

I did love to sing and noticed that every day after lunch, Ray Haas, the student director from the canceled *King Lear*, pulled out sheet music from the lining of his jacket and several students gathered at his table to sing acapella. One day I decided to join them. The group was happy to have another alto who could read music as they had enough sopranos, tenors and basses. Singing madrigals daily was such fun. Ray was two years ahead of me and was also the dining room manager.

The other activity I signed up for was play-reading. Every Tuesday evening Mr. Bart, my seminar tutor, would assign parts to all who signed up. We read one of Shakespeare's plays at each session. A few weeks into the reading, Mr. Bart began to assign larger roles to me. I don't remember who played other parts, but often Ray Haas played my father. He was Shylock, I was Jessica. He was Polonius, I was Ophelia; he played Prospero, I was Miranda. He was Lear, I was Cordelia. I liked and admired this young man. Mostly, however, I went to movies with several other boys, in particular my classmate Don Cummings, a six-foot-four golden haired boy from Pasadena, California. He and

I started studying and working on our homework together, so that we would understand the material better. Soon, though, our relationship morphed into an affectionate one. My dorm had study rooms on the lower floor. With the door closed, the study sessions with Don often ended with lots of kisses. He was very religious, as was I, and for both of us, to remain chaste until marriage was a given.

Our freshman class of 1956 was very large. There were eighty-six of us. Women were permitted entry in 1951, for the first time in the school's 254-year history. Since all classes numbered in the teens, the five sections of freshman class rarely saw one another. All classes were held seminar style, everyone sitting around a table discussing the lessons, learning from one another. I had convinced my high school dancing friend Hildy to join me at St. John's. We were in different classes altogether and I'd see Hildy sometimes in the large gym, when the two of us would play a record and just improvise, dancing and dancing in that huge, beautiful space. I still loved dancing.

Dancing dreams came to me regularly for over thirty years and I wondered if I had chosen the right path. To become a professional dancer, I knew I'd have to remain single and childless. No dancer at that time could marry. But I loved children and wondered even then if I should marry, maybe even have many adopted children.

In 1957, during the spring of my freshman year, I began to experience severe back pain. I consulted with the college nurse and tutors who lived in Annapolis, and received the name of a highly regarded orthopedic surgeon with an international reputation. When my appointment finally arrived, and the exam completed, the surgeon did not present me with good news. He told me my spondylolisthesis had flared up again due to my lower back injury during *The King and I*. The doctor said that unless I had an operation, I would never be able to have children normally and that in my old age I would suffer unbearable pain. He described the operation, which would entail taking out a piece of bone from my leg and fusing the lower spine. That meant I'd most likely be on my back for six months recovering.

I listened to his assessment and realized my dance career was over, and my other dream to have many children might be jeopardized if I don't have the operation. I phoned my mother with the results of the consultation.

Mutti was beside herself, "Katrinchen, you can't. You can't have this operation. You can barely sit still for an hour. How are you going to survive six months on your back?!"

She told me she would look for another orthopedic surgeon and see whether there was a better solution to relieve my back pain.

That summer, mixed in with my other activities, Mutti took me to six doctors carrying the x-rays of my spine to each. That experience revealed to me that doctors were not gods but humans who made judgment calls, which may or may not be correct. Their opinions ran the whole gamut; from one who thought I was the healthiest patient he had ever examined, all the way to the other extreme, one who agreed with the Annapolis surgeon. I have no idea if Mutti had insurance to cover the expense of the doctor visits, but I will be forever grateful to my mother. She must love me after all, I thought. Six months in bed with a fused spine would have killed me. Perhaps it would have killed Mutti as well, for how could she care for me with her own full-time job?

Mutti settled on a surgeon in Baltimore who specialized in healing professional athletes. His solution was painless, inexpensive, and noninvasive. This doctor's cure was for me not to do any exercise for twelve months and to wear a full body brace, which kept my back in a straight line. He said that a year wearing this brace all day would allow new muscles to grow around the displaced vertebra and keep it in place. After a year, all would be well. And even though the brace was quite uncomfortable and I hated not being able to dance for a year, this therapy worked.

Towards the end of the school year, students received a notice saying the ten-dollar lab fee we paid at the beginning of the year would soon be refunded, since no lab equipment needed to be replaced. This notice gave me an idea. What if I collected everyone's lab fee? The total would be about $2,000, which was enough to provide for a scholarship student. The previous fall there had been a revolution in Hungary and many refugees had arrived in the United States. I went to Mr. Tolbert with an idea.

"Mr. Tolbert, if I collect all the students' lab fees, which would amount to around $2,000, could St. John's give it to a deserving Hungarian refugee?" He approved my idea immediately, whereupon I spent all my extra time getting students to sign the form saying they were happy to donate their lab fees for a Hungarian student scholarship. No one turned me down, and the college awarded the scholarship to a bright and talented girl, a recent immigrant to the U.S. In Hungary, she had not been attending school for over a year due to the revolution.

That summer I had a wonderful opportunity to work with children. One of the prospective St. John's students who had stayed with me during the year was Martha Goldstein, and we liked each other right away. When she told me about a summer camp for underprivileged children in New York, I was intrigued. It was run by the Henry Street Settlement, and Martha worked there the previous year and was planning to return. The camp was in Yorktown Heights, a bucolic place in upper New York. They would host children from impoverished families in the lower east side of New York City for two weeks at a time. It was free for these attendees. I got the information from Martha, applied, and got the job.

The first week of the camp was for Jewish kids. Many were Orthodox. All the dishes and food were blessed by a rabbi before each meal. One camper in my cabin told me she didn't like what was being served for breakfast, so I got up early before breakfast started and set out a bowl for her cereal. When I told a friend what I had done, she screamed, "No, no, you can't have a container that uses milk with the other things that are set on the table!" I quickly ran up to the empty dining hall, removed the cereal bowl, and hid it way down in a bench under a giant batch of paper plates and cups.

Besides the children, many of their mothers also came to the camp. I danced for them, saying I didn't know if I should aspire to a career in dance. One lady said to me, "God gave you a talent. You need to use this talent. It was given to you to share, not to keep." That resonated with me.

During a two-day break, before the next group of campers arrived, Mr. Bart surprised me with his visit before leaving for a sabbatical in Italy. He brought his mother to meet me, which seemed unusual. She greeted me warmly and we sat together in the faculty lounge, drinking coffee, and chatting about this and that. Then Mr. Bart and I went for a walk while his mother rested in the lounge.

As we walked, he took my hand. We strolled along the tree-lined streets, talking about his plans to study in Italy. I didn't know exactly how to react. Mr. Bart had spent time advising me about the boys I went to movies with, and he showed me the names of the constellations one starry night. Once, I organized a surprise birthday party for him with several classmates, bringing him cake, ice cream, and small gifts.

He had been a good mentor during my freshman year. He supported me during the don rag, an oral report of the students' progress, where all the tutors sat together and evaluated the students' growth during the semester. There were written report cards that were kept in the office for future reference, but no one ever went to look at their "grades." It was the don rag that was important. During my first don rag, one tutor complained that I was too enthusiastic, and that I would feel things rather than think about them. He wanted me to use my head more than my heart. Mr. Bart disagreed saying there was no reason why I couldn't use both at the same time.

I didn't see anything inappropriate about my friendship with Mr. Bart. In fact, the tutors at the college were all very friendly, and often were seen conversing with students in the coffee shop. But when Mr. Bart showed up at my camp in New York with his mother, an alarm bell rang in my head. Could he be interested in me? He wrote to me often from Italy the following year and sent me an intricately decorative table covering. For my part, I wrote back, telling him more about the boys I was seeing than what I was learning, making certain he knew that I saw him as only an advisor and friend.

Back in Washington, I attended several parties before school began again. At one of them, a Chinese boy who said he was good at fortune telling, looked at the lines on my right hand and predicted that my second son would be famous. I was eager to tell Don Cummings this prediction because he had written me many love letters that summer. Even before the end of our freshman year, we talked about maybe getting married after we graduated.

CHAPTER ELEVEN

Sophomore Year at St. John's

When I returned to campus that September, I was happy to see my friends and to be back at a place that made me so cheerful. I noticed that our class had become a lot smaller. Many of our classmates dropped out for one reason or another. The attrition rate at the time was quite high. Out of our freshman class of eighty-six, only twelve of my classmates graduated in 1960.

When I saw my boyfriend Don, I told him about the friend's predictions I had heard during the summer. "Can we name our second son Ray?" I smiled.

"Your second son will be called Ray Haas, not Ray Cummings," Don said.

"What are you talking about?"

"Katherine, haven't you seen how he looks at you?" I had not, and that he looked at me at all was news to me. Ray was someone everyone looked up to. During the first week each year, the college held elections for president of the student polity. Ray made such an impressive speech that he won by a landslide. He was a brilliant, uncompromising, moral person. Don's comment shocked me. That afternoon I could not concentrate on my homework. Ray looks at me in a special way? How did I miss it? When we sang together every day after lunch with seven or eight others, he never treated me any differently than he did with others. On Tuesday evenings at play readings, I never noticed any special glances when he read the parts. Never. Marry Ray? What a silly notion. I was not in his league.

When the drama club announced auditions for *King Henry VI Part II*, many of us auditioned. I didn't get a part, but Don got the part of Duke of Gloucester and Ray got the part of Cardinal Beaufort. I helped Don with memorizing his lines, and on the night of the performance, I applied his makeup, painting eyes on his eyelids so that in his death scene, as he lay there on stage, it looked like he was staring straight up. It was creepy.

One breezy, late autumn afternoon, on a walk, Don turned to me and said, "Katherine, we're in college here with many other people, but we only spend time with each other. How about we become less exclusive? We'll have plenty of time to be together once we graduate; so for now let's get to know some of our classmates."

I couldn't believe what I was hearing. Was he breaking up with me? He wanted to remain friends, that was obvious. But that's it? I went back to my dorm and spent the evening in tears.

The next day I saw him sitting with the prettiest of our classmates, Dorothy Lutrell. They were happily engaged in conversation. I stormed back to my dorm, grabbed the stack of love letters from Don, dramatically stalked to where the pair was chatting, and tossed the pack to Don.

"Here. Here are your love letters, I don't want them anymore," and I walked off.

Thinking about what Don had said in September about Ray Haas, I decided to try flirting with him. I found a paragraph in my seminar reading that was not clear. Since all the students study exactly the same books all four years, I knew Ray was well acquainted with this passage. He was in the coffee shop, drinking a cup, and reading as I walked up to him.

"Excuse me, Ray," I said, showing him the paragraph I had trouble with in my book. "Can you help explain the meaning of this passage, which I find confusing?" I smiled with my prettiest smile.

He barely looked at me or the passage, "Just read the whole assignment; you'll get it," and he went back to his reading.

That was a bust. But I had another opportunity. A couple of weeks later, a student sat out in the quad playing his bongo drums with an enchanting rhythm. I saw Ray out there on a bench, listening, along with other students and I had the idea to dance over to the center of the quad, improvising to the beats. I danced my heart out, not just to see if he would notice, but because it felt really good to dance. I hoped he liked my dance. Much later I learned that he had been taking photos as I danced.

In retrospect, Don was right: It was too early to be in a serious relationship with another person so I gave up trying to get anyone's attention. I put all my energy into my studies, and in my free time, I learned to fence.

My technique wasn't very good, but I was aggressive, slashing my epee wildly right and left, usually winning against my startled opponent with the sheer determination of my attack. Hildy and I fenced together often. At the spring sports festival, the college gave awards of stylish, elegant wool college jackets to the winners of various sports. Hildy wanted me to win a jacket, so she went around recruiting enough girls to have a fencing tournament in which the winner would receive a jacket. What happened at the competition, however, was that Hildy beat me and she won the jacket. It was perfect because she was the one who worked so hard to put the tournament together. She deserved it, and I was happy for her.

After breaking up with Don and pausing my attempts with Ray, I went out with several young men. Among them was a recent graduate, Joe Cohen. He was tall, dark, and handsome with a gentle, sweet personality. That spring, St. John's had a two-week break. When I shared my plan to spend a week of it at an Episcopal convent in Catonsville, Maryland, Joe seemed quite upset. He asked, "Are you absolutely sure that is what you want to do?"

I told him I had been thinking about my future. I didn't know what God wanted me to do with my life. All the sophomore reading and discussions on the Bible made me think that becoming a nun was what I should do. I had been mulling over this for some time, and I asked our tutor, Winfree Smith, for advice. He was also the priest at St. Anne's Church, where a group of us had a communion service every Wednesday morning at seven. After the service, Winfree made a simple breakfast for us. I also volunteered to teach Sunday school, and there was a darling eight-year-old in my class, Carol Sayre. One day her parents kindly invited me over for a Sunday lunch after church, and I met all of their children, five vivacious young girls. I had always wished to have only boy children, but after that visit, I decided that girl children could be wonderful, too.

One Sunday, I saw a notice on the church program asking for volunteers to visit the nearby jail to comfort the inmates immediately after the service. I volunteered. The first Sunday of each month I visited the local jail and talked to the prisoners. I talked the kind librarian at the college, Charlotte Fletcher, into joining us. When she noticed the piano in the jail, she asked if the prisoners wanted to sing some hymns. They did.

We sang and sang. Then they asked Charlotte to play the music for the Lord's Prayer. Charlotte said it wasn't in the hymnal and she didn't know it well enough to play by ear. So the prisoners sang it acapella. I had never heard non-professional singers sing more beautifully than those inmates. They sang in harmony and we, the volunteers, stood awestruck. They gave us a gift like no other. The beauty of their voices stayed with me, even to this day.

Visiting the inmates was not easy; I didn't know what to say. I couldn't ask them why they were there. We couldn't discuss movies, books, or current events. Most often the inmates would ask me to phone a lawyer, relative, or friend to tell them they'd been incarcerated there. We were told by the jailers that we weren't allowed to do that. I didn't care. I made many phone calls after each visit. I was also appalled at the conditions of the building and the cells. I went to Louis Goldstein, the Maryland comptroller, to protest the conditions.

"We wouldn't put farm animals in a place like that," I told him.

He sat back and told me, "Ms. Hsu, you alone can accomplish nothing. If you want changes made, you have to gather a large group of people and form a committee." I failed, but I think this lesson stayed with me.

One day I was walking on Maryland Avenue outside the campus, and I came upon Ray Haas at Little Campus, a local coffee shop. I went in and sat down with him. We talked about many things, including my plan to spend a week at a convent to see if the nunnery was the place God wanted me to go. He listened to my concerns and walked me back to the college afterwards. Halfway there, in Cumberland Court, he put his hands on my shoulders and kissed me for a long time on the lips. I hadn't expected that and stood there, perplexed, and maybe delighted. We didn't say a word to each other after that for weeks.

On the last day before our spring vacation in April, Joe Cohen offered to take me in his car the next day to the convent in Catonsville, which was about a half-hour drive. That would save me a bus trip and I accepted.

The whole trip there, Joe asked me again and again if I was sure I wanted to spend an entire week there as a postulant, a prospective nun. I told him I needed to see what it was like and that this was the best way to tell. He got the phone number of the convent from me and phoned me every single day I was there, asking how I was.

Life at that convent was tranquil and quietly joyful. The opportunities to speak were limited. There was a convalescent hospital next door full of children who needed long-term care, which was provided by the nuns. I spent an afternoon with the children and taught them songs I had learned the past summer.

At the convent, there was a room where the communion wafers were made in a waffle iron sort of machine. The nun making the wafers prayed continuously as she worked.

One day, I had a session to speak with the instructor of religion and with the Mother Superior. Before the meeting, I was taken for a walk in the woods crossing a stream, stepping on rocks that were not close together. The nun taking me must have done this often, because she laughingly danced over to the other side of the creek and back. It dawned on me that she knew her path in life, and maybe, I had yet to figure out mine.

On the last day of my visit, Mother Superior said to me, "You are young, Katherine. I want you to see the world before you decide to join us. After seeing the world, if it is still your desire to join us, you will be most welcome." She wanted me to grow up, have more experiences, and decide later. I liked what she suggested and took it to heart.

Joe arrived with his car to drive me home to Washington, where my family invited him to stay and celebrate Easter with us. We went to Dumbarton Oaks and hid our colored eggs among the incredible array of blooming forsythias and azaleas. Mutti even hid a box of matzos in honor of Joe's Jewish heritage.

Before the end of sophomore year, all students had to pass a comprehensive test to ensure we were ready for the rigorous third and fourth years. It was the only major test given and I passed, but my good friend Hildy did not. This surprised Mutti, who commented that Hildy was much brighter and a better student than I was.

Students also had to apply for a scholarship by writing a letter to the administration. I wrote that although the college strongly urges students to purchase the great books we read in seminars, so that we could make notes on the pages as we read them, I had so little money that out of the fifty books we read over the last two years, I was only able to afford to buy two: *The Republic* by Plato and Plotinus translated by Stephen MacKenna. That convinced them to award me the largest scholarship I had

ever had. I was moved and thrilled to be able to attend my junior
year at St. John's.

CHAPTER TWELVE

Ray Haas

Once we returned from spring vacation, in early May, I heard rumors that Ray and his two friends, Lynn and Bill, had purchased a sailboat, and they planned to sail to the Virgin Islands right after graduation. Ray spent his free afternoons working on the sailboat, which was docked only a mile or two from the college in Eastport.

The news intrigued me. A few weeks later, I walked down to the pier to see if it was true. Among the many boats docked there, I saw Ray. He was shirtless in his shorts, with tanned and muscled shoulders, sanding or scraping some part of the boat. For the very first time in my life, I thought about making love. I was smitten.

Back on campus, I waited a couple weeks, gathering my courage. If I didn't speak up now, school would end, and I'd have lost my chance. I approached Lynn, one of the boys heading out on this trip with Ray, and asked if I could join them after graduation. Lynn said, "Sure." He must have broached this with Bill and Ray, because the following week a group of students, including Ray, invited me to spend the afternoon on the beach at Sandy Point, which wasn't far from the school, on the Chesapeake Bay. I got my swimsuit and towel and squeezed into the car with the group.

At the beach, I put my towel right next to Ray's. We both lay down on our towels without a word. After about ten minutes, Ray turned to me and said, "What is it you want, Katherine?"

I looked at him and said, "I want to be your wife. I want to have your children. I want to be with you when you want me around and I want to leave you alone when you need time for yourself." He said nothing. I thought about what I'd said and didn't dare stay. I got up and ran into the bay and swam. I kept swimming farther and farther, because I didn't want to come back. How dare I blabber out my feelings like that. I just didn't know what to think, all I knew was that I should not have said what I did.

When the group drove back to the college, Ray walked me over to my dorm, kissed me lightly on my lips and said, "Don't say anything just yet." I did not know what he meant. I was just full of embarrassment and regret. I ran to my dorm and thought about him all night.

Two days later, I was in the tiny Addressograph office, typing name plates when Ray walked in.

"Will you marry me?" he said.

I smiled and looked at him, "Aren't you going to kneel when you propose marriage?"

"I only kneel to God," he answered.

"Are you sure there is a God?" I asked. After all, I barely knew Ray and what he believed in.

He picked up a book and said, "I am more certain that Jesus Christ is the son of God, than I am of this book landing on the floor when I drop it."

"Yes, Ray," I told him, "I will marry you."

"I thought I'd have to spend the morning convincing you, Katherine," he said with his face so happy. "Let's go for a walk."

I wanted to change out of my blue jeans, but he insisted they were fine, and we went for a long walk, and ended up sitting under a large tree on the front campus, kissing passionately, shocking the student body as they walked by. When I asked him why he didn't ask me out on a date if he liked me, he said that he didn't believe that students should date; he was there to get his degree. But, he said, since it was three days before graduation, it was okay to date now.

A cartoon depiction of Ray and Katherine's courtship, as drawn by Katherine's family friend: Katherine sees Ray, she dances for him, and Ray abandons his sailing trip to marry her.

After I told my friends the news, I phoned Joe to tell him I could not attend the dance that evening because I was engaged to Ray Haas. He said, "I will wait for you, Katherine."

No one thought this union would work. Ray and I were opposites in everything, and we barely knew each other. Many girls came to my room to tell me they had had a crush on Ray for years. Several tutors cautioned me not to marry right away and to wait until I graduated. I didn't know why Ray had proposed. But I didn't want him to change his mind, so even though I was really excited about staying at the college for my junior and senior year, I couldn't let this opportunity go.

At about 11 a.m. the next day, Friday, Ray's mother, Mrs. John Haas, and his beloved sister, Edie, arrived from New Jersey for Sunday's graduation. Ray introduced me to them as his fiancée. Their eyes widened with shock.

"Oh," exclaimed Mrs. Haas, trying to seem calm, "how long have you two been engaged?"

I smiled, "Since yesterday, Mrs. Haas."

Edie took over, "We had no idea. How long have you two been going together?"

"Since yesterday," I answered.

They considered this for a while.

"Why don't you join us for lunch? We are just about to leave for a restaurant in town."

I accepted and ran back to the dorm to get ready. But I was terrified and wondered what would happen if they didn't approve of me. What if I forget my table manners? I asked these questions to a friend in my dorm as I fixed my hair in the large dorm bathroom.

"Tell your future in-laws you were a chorus girl!" she said, laughing. That made me feel more relaxed.

At the restaurant both Edie and I ordered shrimp creole. It arrived in a dish with two triangles of toast wedges on the side.

How do I eat those pieces of toast? They were wet with creole sauce and I didn't know whether I should pick them up with my fingers or cut them and use my fork. I decided to watch how Edie ate hers and follow her lead.

The two ladies, however, bombarded me with a thousand questions, and by the time I was ready to eat my lunch, Edie had finished eating her pieces of toast and I didn't see how she'd picked them up.

Ray had worked tirelessly for three weeks on his final essay, which every senior student has to write in order to graduate. Yet it was not accepted, and he was furious. He spent two more days writing some "drivel," as he called it, which was accepted. Since Ray's original essay wasn't accepted, he could not graduate with his class and he would have to wait to receive his diploma on Sunday, by himself, with school president Dr. Weigle and the Dean Jacob Klein (we called him Joshua) presiding.

When the dean announced at the main ceremony, "For the highest academic achievement during all four years, this large silver medal goes to Raymond Haas," everyone waited for one of the students in cap and gown sitting under the Liberty Tree on that breezy afternoon, to get up and accept it. But instead, from the back of the audience came Ray, without a cap and gown, to accept the medal. The audience was perplexed. How could the best student not be graduating? Years later, Ray enjoyed telling this story to others.

On Sunday afternoon, Mrs. Haas, Edie, and I went to Ray's individual graduation under the Liberty Tree.[4] Afterwards, Mrs. Haas and Edie drove back to New Jersey and Ray drove me to D.C. to meet my mom and stepfather, who had just returned from a three-week trip to Europe.

Mutti and Henri were equally shocked at our news. They had met Ray only once for about half an hour a year earlier, during my freshman year. The Broadway play *Inherit the Wind*, with Ed Begley and Paul Muni, was playing at the National Theater in D.C. The manager was my friend from *The King and I*, and I got in touch with him. He told me I could invite as many friends as I wanted and he'd let us all in for free one week-night. I gathered together several people from the college, including Ray, and after the marvelous production, we all drove to my home in Georgetown where my charming mother (without complaining about the late hour) made us snacks before we headed back to the college at midnight.

Before we arrived at my home after Ray's graduation, Mutti called the dean of the college, Jacob (Joshua) Klein. His wife, Dodo, had been Mutti's friend in Germany. Mr. Klein had been Ray's senior advisor and knew him well.

"You want me to describe Ray Haas? Stubborn! Stubborn as a mule. No, no, no, no, stubborn as ten mules!" Mutti wasn't sure what to make of this and waited anxiously to meet him.

Our visit with Mutti went marvelously. Mutti was delighted when Ray sang several German folk songs to her that she knew

---

4The Annapolis Liberty Tree was a tulip poplar that held significance as a symbol of resistance to British colonial power. It was used as a location for meetings and protests during the colonial period. It was felled in 1999, after Hurricane Floyd badly destroyed the tree.

and loved. She was pleased, I think, that he had spoken German as a child to his German grandparents and sang with them. I think she was also thrilled to think that she would not have to support me anymore. I was twenty, the same age Mutti was when she married.

Ray and I talked about our plans to be married that summer after his graduation. He had canceled his plans to sail to the Virgin Islands, and decided to get a job in New Jersey in order to earn some money for our life together. In the fall he was slated to attend Yale Divinity School in New Haven, Connecticut to study theology, which was a seven-year PhD program. I had again promised to work until mid-August at the Henry St. Settlement Camp in Yorktown Heights, New York, so we decided to marry in late August. Because my dream of marrying in Virginia was not allowed, we decided to marry at Christ Church in Georgetown, where I was baptized. I asked Harris Collingwood, my beloved deacon, to officiate at our communion wedding. He said he'd only do it if Ray promised to convert from Unitarian to Episcopalian. Ray declined, so I asked Reverend Winfree Smith from the college, and he was happy to oblige.

Before leaving for my summer job, I went to the marriage bureau to apply for a marriage license where I gave my name as Katherine Elizabeth Hsu. But during the summer, I learned that a person's name on their birth certificate, marriage certificate, and death certificate must all match. So, as soon as my summer job ended, just before my marriage, I rushed back to the marriage bureau to change my name to Leila Barbara Monika. These were the names that my German grandmother had put on my birth certificate back in Berlin, twenty years ago. These names, including my American and Chinese names Katherine Elizabeth

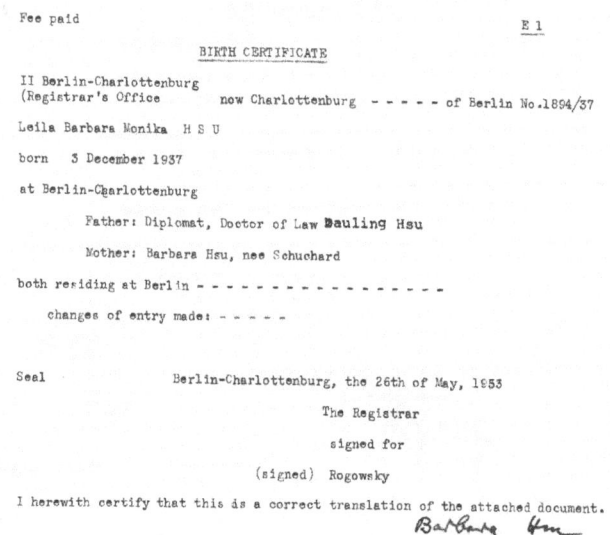

Fee paid E 1

BIRTH CERTIFICATE

II Berlin-Charlottenburg
(Registrar's Office   now Charlottenburg - - - - - of Berlin No.1894/37

Leila Barbara Monika H S U

born   3 December 1937

at Berlin-Charlottenburg

        Father: Diplomat, Doctor of Law **Dauling** Hsu

        Mother: Barbara Hsu, nee Schuchard

both residing at Berlin - - - - - - - - - - - - - - - - -

    changes of entry made: - - - - -

Seal   Berlin-Charlottenburg, the 26th of May, 1953

          The Registrar

          signed for

      (signed) Rogowsky

I herewith certify that this is a correct translation of the attached document.

          Barbara Hsu

Katherine's German birth certificate, which her grandmother filled out

Hsiao Yu Hsu, were featured on my marriage certificate. Ray and I went to New Haven and found a nice apartment near the Divinity School. I asked Ray if we could have lots of children. "We'll have enough," he answered.

Preparing for the wedding was mostly my mother's job, because I was in New York for most of the summer. She asked her good friend Mrs. Bunting if we could use her elegant home and garden, located one block from Christ Church, to hold the reception. She asked me if I'd like to have a musician wearing lederhosen play his accordion during the outdoor reception, but I didn't like that idea. My sister wrote to me from Switzerland (where she, her two kids, and her husband Paul had spent his sabbatical year) and asked if she could sing at our wedding. I said no, and I still regret that. I had been jealous of her my entire life. This was my wedding and I wanted to be the center of attention. Looking back, I should have allowed her the opportunity to shine. She never had a fancy wedding with a pretty, white dress, and lots of guests congratulating her. Plus, her baby Sophie had just died of sudden infant death syndrome and she could have used this chance for some enjoyment.

Mutti and I went shopping for my wedding dress. I loved one that showed my pretty shoulders, a strapless dress that was perfect, but Mutti said that was inappropriate for a church wedding. She chose a high collar, short sleeved dress instead. It had a huge discount because it was yellowed from age. I didn't like it at all, but Mutti did. Later she had it dry cleaned and the yellow hue was eliminated—the dress looked better. But I still wish I could've had the prettier one.

When we were writing invitations for the wedding, Mutti noticed that the majority of our friends were Jewish. Mutti asked me if Ray's family was prejudiced against Jews.

"I don't know, Mutti," I answered, "but I do know that the best man Ray chose is Jim Green, the son of a rabbi." Mutti also chose guests who looked good. She told me she chose different members of the Chinese Military Attaché's Office whose spectacular uniforms fit the bill.

After the dress rehearsal, we invited the party to our house for supper. At first Mutti planned to serve ham but remembering that several members of the wedding party were Jewish, she decided to have another dish that Jews could eat. Ironically, she made a crab dish, not realizing that shellfish was just as forbidden as pork to our Jewish friends.

Once all the guests left our home, Mutti decided to prepare me for married life. The week before, she had sent me to see the family doctor for a physical exam and to prescribe a contraceptive for me. No birth control products were allowed to be sold in Connecticut then. Our doctor told Mutti that I was a virgin, which apparently surprised and pleased her. Her marriage advice for me, delivered the night before my wedding, was only one statement, "It's fun in the afternoon." It fell to my sister Joan to go into excruciating detail about various positions of lovemaking, which, frankly grossed me out.

Because white is the funeral color for the Chinese, the church was decorated in the Chinese wedding color, with red flowers. I needed to choose flowers for my wedding bouquet but I really didn't know much about flowers. I knew I liked gladiolus, so my bouquet was huge, long, heavy, and resembled a baseball bat. When I tossed it at the reception to see which of my young friends would catch it, because of its size and weight, I almost knocked Hildy out.

Several of my old boyfriends were at my wedding: Joe, Hans, Lieutenant Li, and Roger. Mrs. Beatty and David, the little boy I babysat years ago, came. My *King and I* roommate, Aileen, came from New York, as well as friends from St. John's, and Mr. Tolbert and his family. I taught Sunday school when I was a student at St. John's, and one of the Sayre girls was in my class— now the entire Sayre family was at my wedding. My Henry Street Settlement team counselor and good friend Marjorie Noll came from Philadelphia to play the organ for us.

As much as I would have loved to have had my Baba walk the aisle with me, I found that walking with Henri was fine. I had developed much respect for Henri and had even begun to like him. I tripped on my dress again and again. It was too long. We hadn't tried it on. I was overcome with emotion and began to cry. Tears streamed down my cheeks and snot slid down my nose. I tried sniffing, but Joan was right behind me whispering loudly, "Stop it, Katherine. STOP IT." I couldn't wipe my face because my right arm was holding the baseball bat bouquet of gladiolus and my left hand was holding up the skirt of my dress so I wouldn't trip any more going toward the altar. I finally made it there.

During the communion service where the congregation needed to respond to priest Winfree's statements, hardly anyone responded because there were so few Episcopalians in attendance

Katherine and Ray smile on their wedding day. Aileen Passloff is on the right.

who knew the service. All in all, the wedding ceremony was quite a disaster. But the reception was fabulous.

At the entrance of the garden for the reception were two large pillars, which were decorated with two scrolls written in Chinese. My wedding cake had the Chinese character for double happiness instead of a bride and groom on top. Mutti hired our housekeeper, Victoria, to serve the expensive champagne Mutti had bought. Mutti had bought the champagne to outdo her friend, Mrs. Tan Boyu (another German who had married an important Chinese official) by serving better champagne than Mrs. Tan served at her daughter's wedding the previous month. However, Mutti didn't buy a lot of the champagne. When some of my college friends came to Victoria for seconds, she refused to fill their glasses, telling them they already had their share.

Ray and I stayed married, against all odds, for fifty-four years until his death. We changed dramatically during those years. He was initially what one would now describe as a traditional man with conservative values. That is, he believed a man should stand up when a woman walked into the room. He should open doors for her. He should be the main breadwinner. He also believed that a woman should never cut her hair short, nor wear slacks. But as customs changed, so did we. I cut my waist length hair, I wore slacks, and I earned money to support our growing family. We barely knew one another when we first got married, but we discovered how lucky we were not to have guessed wrong. I believe I chose Ray because I saw how Mutti treated gentle Henri. She did whatever she wanted, and complained about his meekness and gentile nature. The eight boys who proposed earlier—Lieutenant Li, Roger, Hans Morsbach, Francois, an Italian cello player, John Chase, Don Cummings, and Joe Cohen—had similar characteristics to Henri. They were mellow and gentle. I turned them down because I worried that I'd be like Mutti with them: short tempered, and domineering. Instead I chose Ray, whose main trait was controlling. He called the shots and rarely wavered. He was not easy to live with, but his other traits, his integrity, his intelligence, loyalty, his sense of humor and great love for me, made living with him a joy.

When I think back to my father's statement back in 1949, "Communism would be a horrible outcome for our country," I now see how right he was. The people in China, under Communist rule, have no freedom of speech nor voting rights, which is of utmost importance in life. I hated the fact that we left China, but being here in the U.S. turned out very well, as it became a place where my mother, my siblings, and I thrived.

Li Jia Tong, my best friend in China when I was eleven, got in touch with me thirty years after I moved, when Joan got a job as a professor in Taiwan. He ran to her office the day she arrived at the university and asked, "Are you Hsiao Yu's sister?" When she said yes, he immediately got my address and sent me a letter and a picture of himself at age eleven just in case I had forgotten him! We corresponded for years and continue to do so; he sent me books he had published in English and took my daughter Carola out for breakfast when she visited Taiwan.

So many things that I thought were disasters at the time turned out to be blessings.

Being treated poorly by cruel racists, classmates, and teachers undermined my fragile ego and shook my self-confidence time and again. But with the consistent kindness of adults and friends I was not only able to regain my confidence, but I became proud of being biracial. And because of the pain I suffered, I was able to recognize that pain in many of the students I taught at summer camps in Vermont and New York, at Solen School on the Standing Rock Reservation in North Dakota, and at Key School in Annapolis, Maryland, and to use that knowledge to support my students and to encourage their strengths.

Missing my rehearsal and being kicked out of Mr. Fokine's company was devastating but ended up to be the best thing for me. I was much better suited as a modern dancer and I finally found dance teachers who valued and believed in me.

Though I never got over Mutti's divorce from my beloved Baba, Henri Noel turned out to be the most loving, patient, and kind step-parent anyone could have asked for.

My Baba suffered after the divorce he didn't want, but then he met and married his student Nancy, and they had two great children. They were a happy family that eventually was allowed to leave Taiwan to live in the United States.

Had I gone to New York to become a dancer as many had suggested, I would never have gone to college, married successfully, or have had my splendid three daughters and a grandchild whom I cherish.

Ray's death was crushing; decades of chain-smoking had wreaked havoc on his health. Numerous operations to relieve his back pain failed. Towards the end, he was in severe pain but he refused to accept morphine from the hospice nurses—and until the last three weeks, he stayed stubbornly in tremendous pain.

He often begged me to end his life. I refused, asking him if he wanted me to go to jail for that crime.

"No," he responded, "you need to do it subtly."

Shaking my head I said, "I've NEVER been subtle in my whole life."

And he sat there for about ten minutes, thinking. Then, lifting his head up with a grin, he said, "I got it, take me to a faculty meeting and bore me to death!"

A week before he died, he felt pain in his chest. "Katherine, I think I am having a heart attack."

Two decades earlier when I was about to take a course on CPR, Ray made me promise never to try to resuscitate him should he have a heart attack, because his own father had died of a heart attack and it was quick and painless. That was how Ray planned to die. Now that he might be really having it, I asked, "Do you want me to do CPR if it really is a heart attack?"

He turned to me, "What does a heart attack feel like, do you know?"

I said, "From what I read, when men have it, it feels like an elephant sitting on one's chest. Now please tell me what I should do if this really is a heart attack?" He thought for a few minutes and answered, "call the zookeeper."

Ray's sense of humor never left him.

I had never lived alone. Our three daughters, all of whom lived in other states, worried about me. Luckily, Ray's hospice provided me with a gifted counselor. Continuing my job teaching fourth graders was a life saver. The parents and colleagues were so supportive that every single evening for three months after Ray's death, parents brought hot meals and their children to my home to eat with me. I could not have imagined a kinder response to my loss. I missed Ray incredibly, but I knew that continuing with his pain, not being able to walk miles each day as he did at his prime made him miserable. He was now at peace.

Little did I realize then that two years later, I would accept the marriage proposal of Bob Feldmann, Ray's young colleague at Key School, who has become the second love of my life.

Throughout our relationship, Ray was extremely protective of me and worried terribly about dying before me. And so when he did, I believe he sent Bob Feldmann over to me.

There were a few things in our fifty-four years of marriage that drove Ray crazy. No matter how hard I would try to be neat, I somehow dropped crumbs everywhere I went without noticing. I would leave little globs of food in the sink instead of scrubbing it out. I often broke things by accident. Ray was the opposite. He was neat as a pin. He never broke anything, and didn't understand why I couldn't be more careful. Bob, on the other hand, drops more crumbs, leaves more globs of food than I do, and is very talented at breaking things. And so, I think Ray sent Bob over to me so that I had someone to compete with my clumsiness. And now I understand why the things I did drove Ray crazy.

Over the years, Ray said that he felt terribly about holding me back. I assured him that I loved taking care of him, that I felt safe and cozy with him around. Now, Bob takes wonderful care of me, as Ray had hoped.

When Ray's good friend asked him a few weeks before his death why he was hanging on with so much pain and discomfort, Ray said I needed him. This friend suggested that I tell Ray he can go. And so I did. I told him I'd be fine.

"Are you sure?"

"Yes, Ray. I plan to marry the day after you die." We both laughed.

Acknowledgments

I am incredibly grateful to my dearest second husband Bob Feldmann who has encouraged my writing since the beginning. He is my first reader and patiently edited everything I ever wanted to publish, spending hours laboring to remove my Chin-glish.

I am deeply indebted to Kelsea Johnson and the Stirred Stories team for believing in me and accepting my manuscript to be published. I feel blessed beyond belief to have Vishakha Darbha as my editor.

I am also thankful to my beloved friends and relatives who cheered me on during this project: they read my manuscript as it was being written and made comments, corrections, and suggestions. Every single reader made it just a little better—and in some cases, a lot better. My niece Beatrice Boepple Mattaway tirelessly went through each revision and made excellent edits, as did my dearest friends Jan Hayes and frenemy Paige Cumberpatch. My friend Max Ochs, with whom I hung out at St. John's College in 1957 and 1958, with his charming wife Suzy, renamed my story as well as the chapter headings, which I liked a lot better. They also made fabulous edits.

My dear friend and neighbor Eloise Baden suggested that I have a pronunciation guide, which was a good idea. Isabel Bratten was the first child to read the first page. She complained that she didn't understand Communism, which made me realize if I were writing this for young adults, I'd better explain politics a little. Isabel's comment was most helpful. My good friend Sandy Kowalczuk helped me send photos to Stirred Stories and helped me proofread the final manuscript.

I thank my dear sister Joan, sweet Angela Kuttner, Maija, and Jia Tong, all of whom helped me with remembering parts of our time together.

For the better part of my life, I had been told by many that I was incapable of writing well, and so I have to thank Lynn Schwartz, my first writing teacher, who taught me how to improve my writing and encouraged me continuously. Her sweet daughter Ibbi cheered me on as well. There's also Vicky Bruce, who thought my little pieces written for Lynn's writing class were good enough to publish in her online newspaper, *The Arundel Patriot*. That kind gesture began my hobby as a wannabe-writer at age seventy-nine. I am deeply indebted to Ruth Glasser, who edited brilliantly everything I published, including this manuscript before I sent it in to Stirred Stories for review. I thank my children: Susan, Carola, and Elijah, who asked about my past and urged me to write my memories down before I wouldn't be able to anymore. This book resembled the making of a soup, with loved ones adding vegetables or seasonings. It took a village to enable me to complete this memoir, and I thank all of you from the bottom of my heart.

About the Author

Katherine Haas was born in 1937 in Germany. Shortly thereafter, her family moved first to Italy, then to China and, when Katherine was eleven, to the United States. Adjusting to new languages and cultures was challenging, and often discouraging. Katherine hopes readers of this book will never be ashamed to be different or an outsider, as she was. She loved raising three daughters with her husband Ray, teaching third and fourth graders for forty-four years, and banding birds. Katherine lives in Maryland with her second husband, Robert Feldmann, who found her as a merry widow in 2014. She spends her retirement having fun learning new languages.

About Stirred Stories

The same stories have repeatedly been told. We're here to stir that up.

We believe that in order to create a truly just society, the stories we consume must be diverse and equitable. That's why we center authenticity and diversity in everything we do, from the books we publish to how we publish them. In short, we're publishing for a better tomorrow.

Follow along with us at www.stirredstories.com.